CONTENTS

PART I

Part II

Part I

1. SWAMI VIVEKANANDA

Vivekananda was born to Visnwanatha Datta and Bhuvaneshwari in Calcutta, on Jan 12, 1863.

The child was called Narendranath. Young Narendra was deeply devoted to God. His devotion was enhanced by mythological stories narrated to him by his mother. Narendra was moved by the misery of the poor and the down-trodden. Compassion was embodied in him since birth.

While studying at college, Narendra met Saint Ramakrishna Paramahamsa at Dakshineshwar and gained his blessing. He devoted his life to serve the master. After the demise of Paramahamsa, Narendra established Sri. Ramakrishna Mission at Baranagar, Calcutta. He implored the youth to imbibe courage and a spirit of adventure. He travelled all over the country. He encountered abject poverty everywhere. Most people lacked food and clothing. Hindu religion was in a state of neglect. Unrest and lethargy were widespread. On reaching Kanyakumari, he swam to a rock in the sea and sat on it in meditation. He contemplated that he had a great task to accomplish. He decided to participate in the parliament of religions held in September 1893 at Chicago, USA. With generous help from the Maharaja of Khetri, he left for America. The maharaja, had borne expenses of his travel.

At the conference, he addressed the gathering as a representative of India by calling them: "My sisters and brothers in America". The audience was spell-bound. Vivekananda's speech on the Hindu religion was profound. Several persons became his disciples. Margaret assumed the name of Nivedita and became his disciple.

On his return to India, Vivekananda established a monastery at Belur, near Calcutta, in the name of Sri Ramakrishna. He worked as the harbinger of a new age. After striving for religious awakening, he passed away on July 4, 1902. He awakened the youth by saying: "Your prosperity is in your own hands. Arise! Awake! Stop not till the goal is reached".

2. MAHATMA GANDHI

Mahatma Gandhi, Father of the Nation, was born at Porbunder in Kathewar state. His father was

Karamchand Gandhi and his mother, Puthali Bai. Karamchand called his son, Mohandas. His mother was a devotee of God. Karamchand was Dewan of Porbunder and Rajkot. Gandhi was born on October 2, 1869.

At a young age, Gandhiji heard stories from the scriptures and mythology through his mother. He grew up with a commitment to truth and honesty. When he was just 13, his wedding with Kasturba was celebrated. After returning from England as a Barrister at Law, Gandhiji went to South Africa to argue the case of Dada Abdulla Sait. There, he was moved by the suffering and violence undergone by Indians. The behaviour of the Whites towards the people of Indian origin was intolerable. Gandhiji established the Natal Indian Congress there. He strove to improve the condition of Indians there.

When he returned to India, Gandhiji was not interested in the practice of law. He started the Satyagraha Ashram near Ahmedabad and lived there. His mind was filled with Sarvodaya ideal. Man should live by truth and non-violence, he said, and preached hatred towards none. Inspired by his lectures, even persons like Vallabhbhai Patel, whose lifestyle was modern, became his disciples.

Leaders like Gopalakrishna Gokhale, Bal Gangadhar Tilak and Lala Lajpat Rai had warned the

British, who were ruling India. Appearance of Gandhiji at such a time to awaken them was almost providential for Indians. He launched non-cooperation stir, civil disobedience, etc.. The Salt Satyagraha had baffled the British. Gandhijl had dared to make salt himself, to oppose tax on it.

Gandhiji was a humanitarian. He opposed untouchability. On seeing caste clashes, he strove to banish differences between the Hindus and the Muslims. He expressed his views in his paper, 'Harijan'. He was sentenced to jail several times for participating in the freedom struggle. He undertook Satyagraha by fasting many times. The entire nation had reposed immense confidence in Gandhiji. Following the "Quit India" movement, there was no alternative for the British, but to granting Independence to India. Gandhiji was arrested then also.

Of course, we attained Independence on August 15, 1947. But India was divided into Hindustan and Pakistan. That triggered communal clashes in the country, causing bloodshed. Gandhiji tried to foster amity between Hindus and Muslims. Gandhiji breathed his last chanting 'Hey Ram' on the evening of January 30, 1948. Nathuram Godse, a misguided youth who presumed that all problems could be solved if Gandhiji was killed, shot him when Gandhiji was approaching a prayer meeting. The Mahatma's demise is not death. Gandhiji is enshrined in the minds of billions of Indians forever.

Gandhiji's philosophy and ideals are valid for all times to come and his life and work are a beacon light for all mankind.

3. HOMI JEHANGIR BHABHA

A famous scientist of India, he was born on October 30. 1909 in a wealthy and well-educated Parsi family of Bombay. Brilliant from his student days, Bhabha obtained his engineering degree from the Cambridge University. He qualified for his Ph.D., in 1934. He conducted research in electricity, Quantum theory. Universal rays, etc., while he was just a student. Bhabha made India enter the age of atom. Thanks to Bhabha's contribution, India could progress in the field of atomic research. Bhabha became the first chairman, when the Atomic Research Centre was established at Trombay near Bombay. The first atomic Centre of the nation under Bhabha's guidance 'Apsara', was commissioned in 1956. In 1945, Bhabha established the Tata Institute of Fundamental Research in Bombay. He served the nation's atomic development programme from 1945 to 1961. Bhabha was a scientist of high standard. He was honoured all over the world in recognition of his services. He was selected a Fellow of the Royal

Society, London, at the young age of 32. Cambridge University conferred the Adam award on him in 1942. He received the Hopkins award in 1948. In 1951, Bhabha was elected President of the Indian Science Congress. He was elected President of the International Conference on uses of atom for peace, held in Geneva in 1955. In 1954, the Government of India honoured him by conferring the Padmabhushan award on him.

Unfortunately, Bhabha died in an air crash in Europe on January 24, 1966.

4. KALIDAS

Kalidas, a great poet and dramatist in Sanskrit, lived in the fourth century A.D. He shone as one of the nine diamonds in the royal court of Chandragupta Vikramaditya, a Gupta King. According to legend, Kalidas was born in a Kuruba(shepherd) family and Saraswati, the goddess of learning, thrived on his tongue by the blessings of Kali. Noted for his similies, poet Laureate Kalidas wrote plays--Abhijnyana Shakuntala, Vikramorvassheeya and Malavikagnimitra and Poetry--Raghuvamsha, Kumara Sambhava and Ritu Samhara. In Ritu Samhara, the poet has portrayed the nature. Meghadoota depicts a message transmitted through clouds by a cursed Yaksha to his beloved. This simple work has been translated into several languages of the world. Raghuvamsha is the story of Ikshavaku kings from Dileepa to Sri Ramachandra. Shakuntala is based on love. This is very well - known and widely translated.

Kalidas lived in Ujjain. Kalidas's poetry will remain as long as the Sun and the Moon last.

5. MOTHER TERESA

Compassion and sympathy are the two invaluable qualities which prompted Mother Teresa to mitigate darkness by lighting a lamp. She was born as Agnes Goxa Bojaxiu on August 27, 1910 at Spoji, Yugoslavia. She was called Mother Teresa after she became a nun in the Roman Catholic Church. Her father was an ordinary professional.

Christian missionaries who came to India in 1921 from Yugoslavia to render humanitarian service, invited people from their country for serving those suffering due to poverty in India. In response to that call, Agnes came to Calcutta. She was then just 19 years. Serving the poor and the sick was her aim. Teresa, who arrived in India on January 6, 1929, did not return to her native land. She dedicated her life to service. Teresa served those who lived on roadside without food and shelter. She strove for their prosperity. When she came to Calcutta, she had Just Rs.five. A priest helped her to occupy a small room. Teresa nursed patients for nine years while staying at that room. Now, thousands of missionary institutions are working with her. Calcutta is the central point of all her activities. Teresa has launched several institutions like the Missionaries of Charity (Sisters) and 'Nirmal Hriday'. Shishu Bhavan is an institution for handicapped and mentally - retarded children only.

Several national and international honours and awards have been conferred on Teresa for her service to humanity. She received the Nobel Peace Prize in 1979. In 1980 the Government on India honoured her by presenting the Bharat Ratna award. She has also received the Jawaharlal Nehru Award for International Peace (1972), Ramon Magsaysay Award (1962) and the Templeton Foundation Award in 1973. Subhashini Das, who was Teresa's first disciple, is Sister Agnes now Mother Teresa is also the Mother-General of the Missionaries of Charity. Mother Teresa passed away on 5th September 1997.

6. C.N. ANNADURAI

People of Tamil Nadu called Annadurai affectionately as Arrinjar Annadurai. Anna Dravida Munnetra Kazhagam, a well-known political party of Tamil Nadu, commemorates him.

Annadurai was born at Kancheepuram on September 15, 1909. He entered politics after obtaining the M.A. degree in 1935. He served Dravida Kazhagam party through his lectures and writings. He was a member of the Rajya Sabha in 1962. In 1967, he contested election as a candidate of the Dravida Munnetra Kazhagam and won to become the Chief Minister of Tamil Nadu. Annadurai was a great thinker, editor of a paper and a famous writer. He rendered exemplary service to Tamil Nadu. He breathed his last on February 3, 1969. The Guiness Book of Records states that cremation of Annadurai was the greatest funeral in the world. About 1.5 million people had participated in it. Annadurai was so immensely popular.

7. JAGAJYOTI BASAVESHWARA

Basavanna was born at Bagewadi in Bijapur district of Karnataka. He lived in the 8th century. Noted for intelligence from his childhood, he studied scriptures under the guidance of Sage Jataveda. Basavanna, who secured a job at the royal court of Bijjala, King of Kalyana, became the Finance Minister by the ruler's grace. He initiated development works for the state's progress. He strove to banish strove to banish superstitions which were deep-rooted among the people. He preached that we should be kind to all animals and shed vanity. He said, discrimination on caste basis should be shunned as all castes are equal. Many people became his followers. Those who detested Basavanna complained about him to the king. But Basavanna's qualities of truth and honesty saved him.

Basavanna established Veerashaiva community to enunciate the principles trusted by him. He admitted people of other castes to his community. He made them to wear a 'linga' as a symbol. He mingled with those who were secluded as "untouchables". 'All of us are the children of Lord Shiva--Shivasharanas', he said.

Basavanna strove to eliminate differences of high and low. Once he tried to arrange an inter - caste wedding. His opponents complained to Bijjala, who conducted an inquiry. Basavanna observed that all human beings are equal in the eyes of Lord Shiva. Caste system is an anomaly. Bijjala did not accept Basavanna's argument. Basavanna did not like to remain there any more. So, he went to Koodala Sangama, a pilgrimage centre, and slept in the Lord there after some time.

Basavanna's sayings are well-known as 'vachanas'. These vachanas in the name of Koodala Sangamadeva are popular.

Why do you set right the world's anomaly

Take care of your own soul

Take care of your own mind

* * *

Don't steal, don't kill, don't utter lie

Don't get angry, don't feel bad about others

Don't praise yourself, don't insult others

This itself is internal cleansing, this itself is external cleansing.

Vachanas like this have thrilled Kannada-speaking people.

8. GAUTAM BUDDHA

Bhagwan Buddha is considered as a reincarnation of Maha Vishnu. Gautam Buddha was born at Lumbini, Nepal in 563 B.C. Shuddhodana, king of Kapilavastu in Nepal, was his father. Mayadevi was his mother. His parents called him Siddhartha. Shuddhodana, who was told by astrologers that the child would become a recluse, brought up Siddhartha within his palace only. Siddhartha was married to Yashodhara, a princess. Raahul was their son.

But, who can alter fate? While on an outing, Siddhartha was disillusioned to see a sickly person, an old man and a corpse. He quit his wife, child, state and palace in search of peace and truth. He visited several places. He discussed the meaning of life with scholars and sages. But he did not acquire knowledge which could convince him. Finally, he meditated under a Bodhi tree at Gaya. He gained enlightenment after meditating for six years.

Greed is the root cause of all human sufferings. It causes sorrow. This was preached by Siddhartha, who later became Buddha. By following the eight paths enunciated by Buddha, man can free himself from botheration of human aspirations. They are: Faith, Thought, Word, Action, Life, Effort, Reminiscence and Prayer. Buddha opposed caste system which was deep-rooted among Hindus. Buddha, who was born on Vaishaka Shukla Poornima day, attained his heavenly abode on the same Vaishaka Shukla Poornima day of 483 B.C.

Buddhism founded by Buddha is one of the main religions in the world. Buddhism is in vogue in India, China, Japan, Burma(Myanmar) and other south-eastern countries.

9. MAHAVEER

Jainism is also a leading religion of the world, like Buddhism. Mahaveer was born in 599 B.C in Kunda

village near Vaishali in Bihar. The child was called Vardhaman. His father, Siddhartha was head of a branch of the Kshatriya dynasty. Trishala was his mother. At the age of five, Vardhaman was joined in a Gurukula. The boy became a great scholar in Sanskrit, and evinced interest in spiritualism. His wedding was celebrated with Yashodhara. A daughter was born. But Mahaveer obtained permission of his brother, Nandivardhan, to go out to gain higher knowledge and observed penance for 12 years. He gained Kaivalya while he was under a tumber tree (Vatice rohasta) on the bank of a river. Vardhaman became Mahaveer then. He was free from the shackles of pain and pleasure.

He propagated the religion conceived by him as Jainism in North India for 30 years. Bindusara, king of Magadha, was among those who applauded his teachings. Mahaveer visited several kingdoms. Though the first Theerthankar, Vrishabha Deva, founded Jainism, Mahaveer shaped it into the present form. He said that non - violence, truth and clean living are necessary. He breathed his last in 527 B.C. at Pavapuri in Bihar. There are several holy places of the Jains in India. Shravanabelagola in Karnataka is a place of piligrimage for Jains.

10. TULASIDAS

Goswami Tulasidas was a great poet of devotional path. He was a Hindu social reformer. Tulasidas was born at Rajapur in Uttar Pradesh. Swami Naraharidas of Kashi brought up and educated him. Tulasidas's wedding with Ratnavali was celebrated. But Ratnavali, to whom he was very conducive, told him to shower his affection on Lord Rama. Since then, Tulasidas became a devotee of Sri Rama. He visited holy places of Sri Rama as a pilgrim.

Ramacharita Manas written by Tulasidas is considered as a superb book and poem. He was a poet of the people. His poetry in Brij language has secured the highest position in Hindi literature. Tulasidas is considered as a symbol of devotion, religion, culture and real knowledge.

Other poetical works by Tulasidas are Bhairavi Ramayana, Geetavali, Vinaya Patrika, Hanuman chaalees and Parvati Mangala.

Tulasidas has depicted Sri Rama as an ideal son, Lakshmana as an ideal brother, Seetha as an ideal wife and Hanuman as an ideal servant. A song, beginning with 'Sri Ramachandra Kripalu Bhajman', by Tulasidas is very famous.

It is believed that Tulasidas, who was born in 1523, lived for 100 years.

11.GURU NANAK

Nanak was born on April 15, 1469 to Mehta Kaloochand and Tripta Devi at Talwandi village, 40 miles off Lahore. People were surprised to see Nanak speak about God by the time he was just five years. By the time Nanak was 15, he learnt Punjabi, Hindi, Persian and Sanskrit languages. His wedding with Sulakshanadevi was celebrated. They had two sons. Nanak was employed for some time. But one day he deserted his kith and kin. None could stop him. He left by stating like a puzzle: "Pardon is my mother, happiness is my father, loyalty to truth is my uncle; these have taken over my mind and senses into their custody. Compassion for animals is my brother. Devotion to God is my son, peace is friend, adventure is daughter".

His goal was Hindu-Muslim unity. Guru Nanak's reputation spread and he travelled all over India. When he reached Delhi, King Sikander Lodhi sent Nanak to jail. But he was released when Babar, a Moghul king and a friend of saints, helped him.

Though a Kshatriya by birth, he studied Hindu and Islam religions in particular and created a condition which excelled both. That is called Sikh. Sikh means disciple. Direct contact between the Master and his disciple is the basic principle of this religion. Nanak's was the path of experience. The base found by him was very simple. Poems composed by him are well- known as 'Japaji'. The fifth birth centenary of Guru Nanak was celebrated in 1969 not only in India, but also in Africa, America, Singapore and other places.

Nanak, who realised God in public service, emancipated several persons and showed them the path of salvation. He breathed his last in 1538.

12. KUVEMPU

Kuvempu is a familiar name to Kannada-speaking people. Kuvempu combines three letters of his name in full, Kuppali Venkatappa Puttappa. Poet Laureate of Kannada and a national poet, Kuvempu is recepient of the Pampa Award instituted by the Karnataka Government.

Kuvempu was born on December 29, 1904 in Tirthahalli taluk. He studied at Maharaja's College, Mysore and qualified for M.A., in Kannada in 1929. He was Assistant Professor, Professor and Vice-chancellor in the University where he studied, before retiring. James Cousins reqfiested Kuvempu who was writing in English, to write in Kannada. Kuvempu's literary exercise which started then, is an eternal fountain. Kuvempu is well-known for his works in all avenues of literature. He is essentially a poet. 'Kolalu', 'Pakshikashi', 'Chandramanchake ba Chakori', 'Panchajanya', 'Prema Kashmira" are some of his collections of poems. 'Chitrangada' is a lengthy poem. ' Jalagara', 'Valmikiya Bhagya', 'Yamana solu', 'Maharatri', 'Beralge Koral' are famous plays by Kuvempu. 'Kanooru Subbamma Heggadathi' and 'Maleyalli Madhumagalu' are novels. Kuvempu is noted for his poems narrating stories. He has also written biographies which are vibrant, and collections of reviews, thoughtful writings, like 'Nanna Gopala', 'Mari Vijnyani', among others.

'Sri Ramayana Darshanam', a work of great poetry, secured the Jnanpeeth award to him. In 1955 this work obtained a prize from the Central Sahitya Academy also. Kuvempu, who was Chairman of the poets' symposium at the Kannada Sahitya Sammelana in Hubli in 1933, was President of the Kannada Sahitya Sammelana in Dharwad in 1957. Kuvempu has been honoured with doctorates from Karnatak, Bangalore and Kuvempu Universities and 'Padma Bhooshana' award from the Government of India. Kuvempu has also been offered felicitation volumes. He has created works which can find a place in world literature.

13. RAVISHANKAR

This famous sitar player of India was born on April 7, 1922. Ravishankar learnt sitar from Ustad Allauddin Khan of Mahiyar. He dedicated his life to play sitar. Pandit Ravishankar is well- known all over the world. He strove hard to popularise Indian music abroad. He has played sitar in the United States of America, Europe and Australia. Ravishankar composed music and conducted an orchestra for a ballet on Nehru's 'Discovery of India'. He was a music director in All India Radio from 1949 to 1955. Music for welcome song of the ninth Asiad held in Delhi in

1982 was composed by Ravishankar. Some Indian universities have honoured him by conferring the doctorate degree. In 1986, the Government of India nominated him as a member of the Rajya Sabha. He became a Fellow of the Sangeeth Natak Academy in 1976. He has won the President's awards twice. Ravishankar, who has started a music school in Los Angeles, is popularising Indian music there. Udayashankar, a famous dancer, was his brother.

Wherever Ravishankar's sitar recital is on, people congregate in thousands. It is so enchanting.

14. LATA MANGESHKAR

Lata Mangeshkar is the most famous background singer of Indian cinema. People will be listening to her music somewhere in the world all the time.

Born on September 29, 1928 in Indore, Madhya Pradesh, she was gifted the divine singing power and a tamboori by her father, Deenanath. She learnt initial lessons in music from her father.

Lata has sung for films along with well-known singers like Mohamed Rafi and Mukesh. She has sung mostly for Hindi movies. She has lent her voice even to a Kannada film. She has sung classical music, Bhajans, devotional songs, romantic songs and patriotric songs. Whichever she sings, it will be melodious. Her singing, which does not lose melody even a bit, has pleased millions of listeners. Leading a religious personal life, she has devoted herself to music by remaining a spinster.

Lata's name appears in the Guiness Book of Records. She has sung over 26,000 songs, it is said. She has sung in all leading languages of India.

The Government of India has honoured Lata with the Padmashree award. She was awarded Filmfare awards several times for singing. The Government of Madhya Pradesh has instituted an annual award of Rs. 1 lakh in her name. It is notable that she has conducted programmes abroad also. (well-known musician M.S. Subbulakshmi is also equally famous)

15. DHYANCHAND

A well-known hockey player, Dhyanchand was born in Allahabad on August 29, 1905. He joined the army at the age of 16. He gained fame as a superb player of hockey. His unique contribution elevated Indian hockey in the world. He was in the hockey team which participated in the Amsterdam Olympics in 1928. The team scored 28 goals, of which 11 were by Dhyanchand alone. He never looked back thereafter. After Independence, Dhyanchand became a major. He was awarded 'Padma Bhushan' by the Government of India. He was honoured with an 'Olive Crown' in the Berlin Olympics (1936). He was then leader of the Indian hockey team which won the gold medal. He scored 101 goals in Olympic games. In other international games, he scored 300 goals. None has excelled this record.

Dhyanchand passed away on December 3, 1979. He has established an institution to impart training to young hockey players.

16. SRINIVASA RAMANUJAN

Ramanujan, who had gained ample knowledge of mathematics, died early. At an young age, he could solve very big problems in mathematics.

He was born on December 22, 1887 at Kumbhakonam in Tamil Nadu. His father was Srinivasa Iyengar and his mother Namagiri Devi. In 1903, Ramanujan completed matriculation. By then, he had studied Trigonametry by Loni and Synopsis of Pure and Applied Mathematics by Kar. He had special interest in mathematics. So, he could not score good marks in other subjects. Unfortunately, he could not complete F.A. examination. He took up a small job for his livelihood. He was married. A Mathematics Professor, V. Ramaswami Iyer and Nellore (Andhra) District Collector, R. Ramachandra Rao spotted his talent in mathematics. Ramanujan's essays were published in the Journal of the Indian Mathematical Society. G.H. Hardy, a famous mathematician of England, read them and immediately invited Ramanujan to the Cambridge University, where he was working. Ramanujan went there in 1914. There he met Littlewood, another scholar. Cambridge University conferred the honorary B.A. degree on him in 1916. But he returned to India in 1919, unable to cope with the weather there. Many institutions tried to arrange for treatment to him, with a desire to maintain contact with him. But Ramanujan passed away on August 20, 1920. He was 32 then.

Ramanujan's talent in numericals was exceptional. He could define and give formula of any number. When Hardy went to hospital to see Ramanujan, he said that the number (1729) of the taxi by which he came, was not good. Ramanujan shot back: "Don't say like that. It is an excellent number. 1729 is the smallest number among total in solid form that can be said of double numbers in two ways". When Hardy calculated on returning home, it was proved. $1729=12^3 + 1^3$ and 10^3+9^3. This illustrates Ramanujan's talent.

17. ACHARYA VINOBA BHAVE

Harbinger of the Bhoodan movement, Vinoba, was born at Gagode village in Colaba district of Maharashtra on September 11, 1895. His father was Narahari Shambhurao and his mother, Rukmini Devi. His parents called him Vinayaka. Mama Phadke called him Vinoba. Saints are called by adding 'Ba' at the end of their names.

Vinoba received religious education at his home.

At school, he used to spend much time in the library. After matriculation in 1917, he joined a college. But the educational system there disappointed him. He met several scholars at Kashi (Banaras). Later, he lived in Sabarmati Ashram run by Gandhiji. In 1921, Gandhiji deputed Vinoba to Wardha for establishing Satyagraha Ashram, as desired by Jamnalal Bajaj. Vinoba established the Ashram and undertook several constructive tasks.

Vinoba dreamt of the 'village-state'. Every village should be independent and strive for its prosperity. It should produce goods required by a family there itself to the extent possible, he said. His final goal was to create a Sarvodaya society by converting society through Bhoodan. Stating that "land belongs to all; those who own it should give it to others", he took up the task of distributing land donated by landlords. Bhoodan movement of Vinoba attracted people's attention.

Bhagwad Gita was Vinoba's favourite. When he happened to be at Dhulia jail, he wrote an invaluable volume, Gita Pravachana, in Marathi. This is a work of repute.

Vinoba was sentenced to jail term thrice for participating in the freedom struggle. He participated actively in the flag Satyagraha held at Nagpur in 1923 and in the Satyagraha held at Vaikom in Kerala in 1924. He spent his last days at the Wardha Ashram amidst his disciples. Vinoba was a brave man who invited his death. He was sore at the happenings in the country. He died at the age of 88. Subsequently, the Government of India honoured him by conferring on him Bharat Ratna award. A social reformer, Vinoba, was like a teacher to the world.

18. B.K.S. IYENGAR

The life and works of Yogacharya B.K.S. Iyengar are of epic proportions. He was born on December 14, 1918, in Karnataka in a large and poor family. At the early age of fifteen, he went to Mysore. He was initiated into Yoga by his brother-in-law Prof. T. Krishnamacharya, who was a well known yoga Scholar. During 1937-40, he worked as a Yoga instructor at the Deccen Gymkhana at Pune. He started teaching Yoga privately in Pune. In 1943, he married Smt. Ramamani. In 1948, he taught Yoga to Sri J. Krishnamurthy. He was conferred the title of 'Yogi Raja' by Swami Sivananda of Rishikesh. He taught Yoga to many distinguished personalities of National and International repute.

In March 1952, the celebrated Violinist Yehudi Menuhin, became Iyengar's student of Yoga. Sri Iyengar has travelled extensively to all corners of the world to promote Yoga. In 1954 he started his Yoga Classes in Bombay. In 1976, Iyengar gave a memorable lecture demonstration at the Harvard College, Philadelphia. He participated in the Festival of India at London. There are over 170 Iyengar Yoga Centres all over the World. In 1991, he was conferred with the 'PADMA SHRI' Award. His famous Books include, The Light on Yoga, Light on Pranayama, The Art of Yoga, Light of Yoga Sutra of Patanjali. In 1973, his wife passed away, Ramamani Iyengar Memorial Yoga Institute at Pune is serving not only as the foremost seat of Yogic learning but also as a centre for Yoga Pilgrimage.

19. CHAKRAVARTHI RAJAGOPALACHARI (RAJAJI)

Rajaji was a genius who participated in India's freedom struggle and served the country by assuming several posts in Independent India. Rajagopalachari was born on December 9, 1878 at Torappalli village in Salem district. Chakravarthi Iyengar was his father. Chidambarammal was his mother. He studied at Hosur, (Tamil Nadu) and Bangalore. After obtaining a degree in law, he started practising as a lawyer. India was ruled by the British then. Mahatma Gandhi had launched a student struggle for liberating India.

Rajaji was elected the first Governor-General of Independent India in 1947. He later also became the Chief Minister of Tamil Nadu. Due to differences of opinion in the Congress party, he relinquished it and launched his own party called the Swatantra Party.

Rajaji was a good writer. Ramayana, Mahabharata, Bhagwad Gita, stories of Upanishads, Avvaiyar and other works by him are popular. With a good command over Tamil and English, he was an excellent speaker. People were gathering in large numbers to hear his lectures.

Rajaji passed away on December 25, 1972 at Madras when he was 95 years old.

20. SUBRAHMANYA BHARATHI

Subrahmanya Bharathi's name is notable in Tamil literature. Songs composed by him in easy style are popular even now. Born and dead during India's freedom struggle, he dedicated himself to service of the country. He was a poet not only of Tamil Nadu, but of entire India.

Bharathi was born on December 11, 1882. His father, Chinnaswami Iyer, was a machinist. He wanted his son to become a graduate. Bharathi studied at a high school at Tirunelveli. Education in English was given importance then. But he did not like it. He questioned whether he should seek a job by studying history of some other country. He did not want that type of education. Nature itself was his school. Animals and birds, hills and forests, rivers and water, man and God were subjects dear to him. He was married to Chellammal at the age of just 15 years. He appeared for the entrance examination at Varanasi. He joined the Ettiyapur King's court as a poet and adviser. Yet, due to his independent mind, he could not continue in that job. He worked as a teacher for some time. Later, he became a journalist. He worked for newspapers, Swadeshamitran and India. Later, he started an English periodical called Balabharathi. In 1905, he particiapted in the Congress session at Kashi presided over by Gokhale.

Bharathi's articles and patriotic lyrics were unbearable to the British, who were then ruling India. Preparations were made to arrest him. Bharathi moved to Pondicherry, which was ruled by the French. There he met Aurobindo, V.V.S.Iyer and others. But he did not like to remain incognito there. He became a sub- editor of the Swadeshamitran in Madras. After meeting Gandhiji there, he composed a song on Gandhiji and sang it. He wore a thick moustache, a headgear like Sikhs and a shawl on his shirt to hide his identity. He was upset over people's attitude that Harijans should not be touched. He mingled with Harijans. He wrote: "Jartinooru solluvai po po po", denouncing those who made caste differentiation. He wrote patriotic songs for children in the name of "Papa Pattu". He wrote stories, poems, reviews etc. Tamils honoured him by calling him 'Bharatiyar'. He wrote mini- poetry called Kannam Pattu, Panchali Shapatham and Kuyil Pattu in Tamil.

Bharati died on September 12, 1921 due to a temple elephant's fury. Though he died young, his poetry has made him immortal. His love for freedom is a source of inspiration to all Indians.

21. K. KAMARAJ

It is no joke to be born in a poor family and to become one of the leaders of India without much education. Kamaraj Nadar has done it!

He was born at Viruduppati in Tamil Nadu on August 15, 1903. His father was Kumaraswami and his mother was Shivakami Ammeyar. Kamaraj studied up to the sixth standard. Later, he dedicated himself to the service of the country. He participated in the movement to boycott foreign goods in 1920. He was imprisoned several times for participating in the freedom struggle.

He was a leader of the Congress in Tamil Nadu. In 1954, he became the Chief Minister of that state. He formulated the 'Kamaraj plan'. As a result, he relinquished Chief Ministership. As President of the All India Congress Committee, he solved many problems confronting the country. Kamaraj's handling of the affairs of the party as a seasoned politician when Jawaharlal Nehru and Lal Bahadur Shastri passed away, was widely appreciated.

Kamaraj breathed his last on October 2, 1975. In

1976, the Government of India honoured him with 'Bharat Ratna'.

22. JAGDISHCHANDRA BOSE

Jagdishchandra Bose, who shone like a star in the sky of science, was an eminent scientist of India. "Even plants have life. They live like us. They also consume food like human beings. They sleep at night and are awake early in the morning. They also experience pain when beaten up. Even they have birth and death". Bose was the first scientist to make the world aware of such knowledge.

Bose was born on November 30, 1858 at Faridpur in Dhaka district, now in Bangla Desh. His father, Bhagwan Chandra Bose, was a high-ranking officer of the government. He had admitted his son to an ordinary school, as he wanted him to treat all with equality. He picked up stories and poems from his mother in childhood. As a result, he cultivated patience, loyalty and adventurism, which a scientist should have. Bose graduated after studying in St. Xavier's High School and College, Calcutta. In 1880, he went to London and studied botany and medicine. Lord Rele was his guide.

After returning to India, Bose conducted scientific research. Though he did research related to electricity at first, research conducted by him on plants made him famous. By administering an injection to a plant, he proved that plants either wriggle or die when poisoned. To show reactions in plants, he devised sophisticated equipments. The Royal Society of London invited him to deliver lectures and conferred its Fellowship on him. A research institute established by Bose in Calcutta in 1912 is functioning even now. An admirer of literature, he was a friend of world-renowned poet Rabindranath Tagore. Bose has written volumes such as "Reaction in actives and inactives" and "Plant reaction".

Bose, who passed away on November 23, 1937, was a great scientist who shone like a bright star.

23. SALIM ALI

World-famous ornithologist Salim Moyijuddin Abdual Ali was born on November 12, 1906. He was fond of nature from his childhood. Somehow, he did not obtain a degree from any university. Nature was his school. When he went to Burma to help his brother, he roamed in forests there listening to chirping of birds and watching at their colour and flight.

After returning from Burma, Salim Ali studied zoology and joined the National History Society, Bombay, as a guide. He underwent higher training in Germany. But when he returned to India he had lost his job. By paying whatever money he had, he bought a house on the sea coast in Bombay. His wife managed the household with her earnings. Ali who was fond of birds from his early days, studied bottle-birds (ploceus baya) and published articles on it in 1930. They helped Ali to become a noted ornithologist and fetched honour and recognition to him. By studying birds in Kumaon Hills, he gained fame all over the world.

Salim Ali has written books on different birds. "The book of Indian Birds" is a unique volume. He has named in this book different kinds of birds along with their pictures. Even a layman can identify a variety of birds, by seeing those pictures. In 1948, he brought out a unique work-- "Handbook of Birds of India and Pakistan" in 10 volumes, along with S. Dylan Ripley, another ornithologist of international recognition. Salim Ali travelled all over the country in search of birds. His yearning for birds even in old age was amazing.

Several awards and honours were conferred on Ali. The Government of India honoured him by nominating him as a member of the Rajya Sabha. He has narrated his life in the company of birds in his autobiography, "Fall of a Sparrow".

Salim Ali passed away on June 20, 1987 in Bombay.

24. B.R. AMBEDKAR

Bheemrao Ambedkar was born as the 14th son of Ramji at Ambavade village in Ratnagiri district of Maharashtra. Born on April 14, 1891, his full name was Bheemrao Ambedkar. Even while studying at school, he happened to know the feelings of the high and the low which was deep-rooted in society and felt very bad about them. His teacher, who was impressed by Bheemrao's brilliance, gave his surname to him and told him: "henceforth your name is Bheemrao Ramji Ambedkar". From that day, Bheemrao Ambavadekar became Bheemrao Ambedkar. Ambedkar studied at the Elphinstone College, Bombay and obtained his B.A., degree. He secured a job under the Maharaja of Baroda, went to America and returned to India in 1917 with his Ph.D. He secured a top job. Later, he went to London and returned as a Barrister.

Ambedkar had decided to abolish untouchability which had thrived for centuries. It was said, "untouchables" should not use water from a tank in Colaba district, Maharashtra. Ambedkar used that water himself first and propagated the principle that all are equal. His sharp mind had begun to exert itself from the time he was not allowed to sit along with other students in the class in his childhood, as he was born a Mehar. After some days, in defiance of a prohibition to enter a temple, he entered Veereshwara temple and said that those who are called as "untouchables" can enter the temple and also drink tank water. A case was filed against Ambedkar in the court, which ruled that tanks and wells are public properties.

Participating in the round table conference in 1931, he spoke for the "untouchables" who were called Harijans and argued that they should also be allowed to exercise franchise and the right to elect their own leader.

When India gained freedom on August 15, 1947, Ambedkar became the first Law Minister. He assisted in formulating the Constitution of India. He served as chairman of the Constituent Assembly. On November 1, 1949, the government accepted the draft of the Constitution and called him the 'Modern man of India'. Ambedkar devoted his life for the emancipation of Harijans.

Ambedkar became a Buddhist for peace of mind and participated in the Buddhist conference in Sri Lanka in 1950. He was fond of books. Once he brought 2,000 books bought in New York. He also wrote some books. People affectionately called him "Baba Saheb". Ambedkar, who strove to banish the caste system, was conferred several honours. He passed away on December 6, 1956. The nation celebrated his birth centenary on a grand scale. The Government of India conferred on him "Bharat Ratna". His birthday is being celebrated with enthusiasm all over the country now.

25. C.F. ANDREWS

Andrews, who was born in Europe, came to India in 1904 as a British Missionary. After living here for a long time, he delved into the freedom struggle and worked closely with Indian leaders. He became an Indian and was honoured as a "Deenabandhu". He died in Calcutta in 1940.

26. CHANDRAGUPTA MAURYA

Chandragupta, who was born in 322 B.C., was the founder of the Maurya dynasty which was India's first historical kingdom. A talented statesman, Chanakya (Kautilya) was at his royal court. Chanakya was not only Chandragupta's teacher, but also his minister, later. With Chanakya's advice and co-operation, Chandragupta won Magadh Kingdom by forcing the Greeks flee Punjab. In 305 B.C. he defeated Selucus, a Greek. Megasthanes, ambassador of Selucus, had not only visited Chandragupta's royal court, but has also provided invaluable information on that period in his book "India". It is said that Chandragupta Maurya had come along with sage Bhadrabhahu to Karnataka and settled down at Sravanabelagola. Chandragupta is presumed to have lived till 289 B.C.

27. SIR TEJBAHADUR SAPRU

A famous advocate and scholar, Sir Tej Bahadur was a member of the Imperial Legislative Council from

1916 to 1920. For the next three years, he was a member of law section in the Viceroy's Council. He has the reputation of participating in all the three round table conferences during the British rule. He was very much responsible for the Gandhi-Irwin agreement of 1931 and the Poona pact of 1932.

28. SIR C. V. RAMAN

Nobel laureate Sir C. V Raman was born at Tiruchirapalli on the banks of the Cauvery on November 7, 1888. His father, Chandrasekara Iyer, was a teacher and scholar. Parvati Ammal was his mother. Sanskrit and music pervaded their home. It was a confluence of intellectuals. Raman had a good and congenial environment from childhood. After passing all stages of education in first class, Venkataraman bagged a gold medal in B.A., He loved science even as a boy. German scientist Helmolts and voice scientist Lord Raleigh influenced him. He even passed the I.C.S. examination.

In 1907, Raman married Lokasundari. He also secured a job at the Accountant-General's office in Calcutta. But he took up research in an institute at Calcutta, because of his curiosity. He was fond of teaching science. He became the Secretary of the

National Institute for Cultivation of Science. He wrote articles explaining responses in musical instruments like violin, mridangam and tabla. He visited England for sometime and spoke at the Physical Society of London. After returning to India, he wrote research articles and contributed them to the Royal Society, London. Foreign scientists applauded his articles. In 1924, Raman became a Fellow of the Royal Society. In 1925, he went to Russia to receive an honour from the Russian Academy of Sciences. In 1926, he launched the Indian Journal of Physics. For some time, he was also a professor at the Services College, Calcutta.

Astounded by the beauty of the seas, Raman thought over its blue colour. Was it due to the sky's blue? Rays of the Sun is composed of seven colours. He observed that the Sun rays is spread when passed through a transparent object. He studied light's frolic. Rays of spread light are called "Raman rays". "Raman's effect" helped very much in higher study of Physics. His research on his own "Raman's effect" secured him the Nobel Prize of the Swedish Academy of Sciences. The then Government of Mysore granted him 24 acres of land for conducting research. Raman Research Institute was started by him in Bangalore. Raman was very much interested in collecting objects. He was collecting flowers, musical instruments, stones, diamonds, etc., The Government of India honoured him with Bharat Ratna award in 1954. Science alone was his God and religion. Raman was saying that his life was reserved for science. His life was like that of a sage. He passed away on November 21, 1970, at the age of 83.

29. SIR M. VISVESVARAYA

MV exclaimed, "Oh! how much water is being wasted!", when he saw the world-famous Jog falls. His dream came true. A dam was constructed across the Sharavathi river which originates and flows in Karnataka. Water stored there was used to run power generators at the Sharavathi power station. The country gained valuable electricity needed much for the homes and factories. Sir MV was the engineer who dreamt of this project.

MV was born on September, 15, 1861 at Muddenahally, Chickballapur taluk, Kolar District, in a poor family. His father was Srinivasa Sastry and his mother, Venkachichamma. Visvesvaraya did not hesitate to study in spite of poverty. He studied very hard. In 1875, he continued his education at the high school by going to Bangalore on foot. He earned some money by offering tuition at homes. After completing B. A. in 1881, he became an engineer after studying at the Pune Engineering College with a scholarship. He joined service as an engineer in the Bombay province and became a Chief Engineer in about 14 years. He was noted for arranging drinking water and sewerage in Pune. He went abroad to study technology in industry, irrigation, generation of electricity, etc., there. He advised on supplying drinking water to Aden city.

After returning to India, as requested by the Nizam of Hyderabad, Visvesvaraya helped to prevent havoc caused by flood of the Moosa river. Krishnaraja Wodeyar IV, the then Maharaja of Mysore, invited him and appointed him as the Chief Engineer. He also served as the Dewan of Mysore and strove hard to provide a modern look to Mysore. As a result of his intelligence, Krishnaraja Sagara Dam, Bhadravathi Iron and Steel Works, Bhatkal Port and Mysore railways took shape. He delved into several social services also. The State Bank of Mysore, Kannada Sahitya Parishat and Grama Panchayats are all his achievements.

Visvesvaraya was well-known mainly as an engineer. In 1955, the Government of India conferred the Bharat Ratna award on him. In 1960, his birth centenary was celebrated in Bangalore with gaiety. A postage stamp bearing his portrait, was released. In recognition of this eminent engineer of India, his birthday is being celebrated in the country as "Engineer's Day".

30. DR. S. RADHAKRISHNAN

Dr. Sarvepalli Radhakrishnan was a great thinker of India and an ideal teacher. He encouraged education in letter and spirit.

He was born on September 5, 1888 at Tiruttani in Chittoor district of Tamil Nadu, in a middle class

family of religious attitude. He studied at the Christian College, Madras and was a disciplinarian in his life. He wrote a paper on the "Moral principles of Vedanta" for his post-graduate degree in philosophy. After securing his M.A., degree from the Madras University, he was appointed as the Professor of Philosophy in the Presidency College. In 1918, he joined the Maharaja's College, Mysore and taught philosophy for some time. He was well versed in Telugu and English, besides Hindi and Sanskrit.

Radhakrishnan was able to discuss Vedanta in a scholarly way. One of his books is "Importance of Religion in Philosophy". After writing this book, he went to Calcutta university and served there as a Professor. He also served as Vice-Chancellor of the Andhra and Kashi Universities. Delivering lectures was his forte. His style and command over the subject was exceptional.

In 1952, he was elected the Vice-President of India. He was elected the President when Dr. Rajendra Prasad, who was the first President of India, relinquished his office in 1962. He served in such a way that made India a most honoured nation in the world.

Dr. Radhakrishnan stepped down in 1967. He passed away in April 1975. In 1953, the Government of India honoured him with the Bharat Ratna award. His birthday is being celebrated all over the country as Teacher's Day on September 5 every year.

31. JAWAHARLAL NEHRU

Jawaharlal Nehru was born on November 14, 1889 at Allahabad as the only son of noted lawyer, Motilal Nehru and Swaroop Rani. Motilal sent his son, who was very bright, to England. Nehru obtained his M. A. degree from the Cambridge University and after completing the barrister examination, returned to India. He married Kamala, a great patriot.

Nehru resented subjugation of India by the British. Although he started work as a lawyer like his father, he participated in the struggle for freedom under Gandhiji's influence. Participating in the All India Congress Committee sessions, he declared that India should be prepared for all sacrifices to win freedom. For participating actively in the freedom struggle, he was imprisoned several times. As a result of the struggle, India gained freedom on August 15, 1947.

Nehru was elected the first Prime Minister of independent India. He wanted that India should be developed and shine brightest among all nations. He strove hard during his term of office to make India an honoured nation in the world. He specially supported scientific and technological progress. He established the Sahitya Academy and the Book Trust to nurture art, literature and culture. He enunciated the principle of Panch sheel. Its five tenets are: honouring mutual security and sovereignty, non-interference by one country in the internal administration of another, safeguarding mutual equality and interest, mutual non-aggression and peaceful co-existence.

Nehru was a talented writer. His two books "Discovery of India" and "Glimpses of World History" are world-famous.

Nehru dedicated his life to our country's independence. He worked for the progress of the country even after independence. In 1955, on behalf of the entire country, the President honoured Jawaharlal Nehru by presenting him with the Bharat Ratna award.

Nehru was stunned by the Chinese aggression on India in 1962. His health deteriorated subsequently. Nehru breathed his last on May 27, 1964. Nehru's birthday is being celebrated as Children's Day, as desired by him.

32. RABINDRANATH TAGORE

Gurudev Rabindranath Tagore is the most famous poet of India. He was a novelist, playwright, philosopher, educationist, freedom fighter, actor and artist. His was a versatile personality.

Rabindranath was born on May 7, 1861 in Calcutta. Devendranath was his father. Writing poems was his hobby from childhood. His writing was vast. "Gitanjali" is his well-known collection of poems. Nobel prize was awarded to this work of his on November 13, 1913. He has written Bengali novels like Gora, Naukaghata, Vibha Raja aur Rani, and Muktadhara, as well as famous stories like Kabuliwallah and Kshudit pashan. "Janaganamana" written by him is the national anthem of India.

Rabindranath established an international institution of education called Shanti Niketan at Bolpur in West Bengal in 1901 to forge a universal culture mixing values of both the East and the West. Later, it developed as the Vishwa Bharati University. In recognition of his services, the British Government honoured him by conferring the knighthood ("Sir"). But after the Jalianwalabaug massacre in Amritsar in 1919, he returned that honour to the British Government.

Tagore passed away on August 8, 1941 at the age of 80. Honoured as a world poet, he was a proud son of India.

33. INDIRA GANDHI

Indira Gandhi was the only daughter of Jawaharlal Nehru. She was born on November 19, 1917 in Anand Bhavan at Allahabad. Nehru was an admirer of Ashoka, who was also known as Devanamapriya Priyadarshini. So he called his daughter as Indira Priyadarshini.

Indira grew up as the beloved daughter of the Nehru couple. Indians were ruled by the British then. Nehru had to go to jail after participating in the freedom struggle. Kamala Nehru used to be continuously sick. Indira grew up in such a situation. Even her education did not continue unhindered in the same school. For some time, she studied in Switzerland.

Freedom lovers used to throng Anand Bhavan always. Indira was the favourite of her grandfather Motilal. Environment made Indira an astute patriot in future. Nehru wrote letters to Indira from jail, in which he elucidated the history of India. They helped her to know about her country. Her wedding was celebrated with Feroze Gandhi. She went to jail along with her husband by participating in the "Quit India" movement of 1942.

India won freedom in 1947. Indira Gandhi worked by participating actively in the nation's politics, like her father. In 1966, following the death of India's premier, Lal Bahadur Shastri, Indira Gandhi was selected as the premier and assumed charge of the country's administration.

Indira Gandhi implemented the policy of banks' nationalisation, 20 - point programme, abolition of privy purses to princes, etc. She gave priority to development of science, exploration of space, generating electricity, irrigation, removal of poverty, etc.

Power was not a bed of roses to Indira Gandhi. Punjab and Assam problems turned formidable. She also had to struggle against those who wanted to found "Khalistan" state. She had to fight those who hid arms in the golden temple at Amritsar and indulged in acts causing loss of public property. When the army entered the golden temple, terrorists became furious and conspired to assassinate Indira Gandhi. She did not lose heart. She dedicated her life to the nation's integrity.

When Indira Gandhi was proceeding to her office from her residence on the morning of Wednesday, October, 31, 1984, assassins killed her by showering bullets from between bushes. The entire world condoled her death. The day of her killing is being celebrated as the National Unity Day.

34. SUBHASHCHANDRA BOSE

Subhashchandra Bose struggled risking his life in his own unique manner for India's freedom. Honoured

as Netaji, he hailed from Bengal. He was born on January 23, 1897 in Cuttack, Orissa. Janakinath Bose was his father and Prabhavati his mother. He began to learn English at the age of just five years. He was very brilliant and passed the B.A. examination in first class. As desired by his father, he appeared for and passed the Indian Civil Services examination conducted by the British Government. But as he did not like to work under an alien rule, he resigned his civil service job and jumped into the freedom struggle.

Subhash became an active member of the Congress. But since Gandhiji's principles and policies were not acceptable to him, he quit the Congress party and indulged in revolutionary activities. As a result, he was imprisoned several times. He did not lose courage. On January 15, 1941, he went to Japan after escaping from jail and formed the Indian National Army (INA) in 1943 with the help of the Japanese. His stance was that Independence should be gained by waging a struggle with the help of an army. But other leaders of the country had been saying that India should gain freedom through peace and non-violence.

In 1945, the I.N.A. invaded India from the north-west of the country under the leadership of Bose. But this attempt did not succeed. Yet, this motivated the British to think of granting freedom to India soon.

It is presumed that Bose died in an air crash on August 17, 1945. Dedicating himself to the country, he was saying: "Give me blood, I will get you freedom". "Jai Hind" was the slogan offered by Bose to Indians.

35. TANSEN

Tansen was a famous musician of India. According to legend, lamps used to light up when he sang the Deepak raga. He was born in 1506 in Gwalior. It is said that having born in a Brahmin family, he adopted Islamic religion. Haridas was his teacher. Tansen learnt music excellently and became a well-known singer. This was noticed by the Moghul ruler, Akbar. As he was a famous patron of art, he made Tansen the music exponent at his royal court. Tansen was one of the nine gems there. Being in the royal court, Tansen was able to compose new ragas based on classical music. He forged friendship with Soordas, noted devotee of Lord Krishna. Tansen used to derive happiness by singing bhajans and devotional songs along with Soordas. Once, Tansen suffered defeat in a competition with Baiju Bavra, another well-known singer. This inspired him to become a devotee of Lord Krishna. Tansen was a poet also. He died in 1589 at Behat, his native place. His tomb is situated there. Every December, a music convention is held in honour of Tansen at Behat.

(Other noted singers, composers and writers of Dasa literature are: Thyagaraja, Purandaradasa, Kanakadasa, M.S.Subbulakshmi, M.L.Vasanthakumari, M. Balamuralikrishna, Bhimsen Joshi and Jesudas)

36. J. KRISHNAMURTHY

Jiddu Krishnamurthy was a famous thinker of our country. He is equal to a pontiff. He was born in 1895 in a Brahmin family in Madras state. When he was only 11 years, his father had taken him to Annie Besant, who had founded the Vedanta Society. Krishnamurthy obtained good education in the better environment of the Theosophical Society.

In 1929, he severed contact with the Society and toured all over the world. He went on elucidating the real meaning of truth, through his scholarly lectures. He was saying that we should give birth to a new man. To him, the entire life was full of meditation. Krishnamurthy had no faith in either customs or prayers. People all over the world were aspiring to listen to his lectures. A bachelor throughout his life, he was a prominent writer also. His books on topics of Vedanta have attracted attention of intellectuals. He passed away on February 17, 1986 in America. The world knows J. Krishnamurthy as a great philosopher and teacher of Vedanta.

37. ASHOKA MAURYA

Ashoka was the son of Bindusara, the Maurya Emperor. Born in 294 B.C., he ascended the Magadha throne in 273 B.C. He also aspired to extend his state like earlier kings and annexed several states. But he was terribly upset on seeing bloodshed in the battle against a powerful state like the Kalinga kingdom. He converted himself forthwith and embraced Buddhism which was in vogue then. Being highly religious minded, he propagated Buddhism. Prosperity exuded in his state. He never waged a war after the Kalinga war. He ordered planting of trees on both sides of roads for shade. He constructed shelters for tourists and hospitals for treatment of the sick persons and animals. He showed compassion for the poor. He was called Devanamapriya Priyadarshi.

He stopped hunting of animals. He gave up non-vegetarian food and prohibited killing of animals for food. He sent his daughter Sangamitra and son Mahendra for propagating Buddhism up to Sri Lanka. Further, he appointed preachers in countries like Syria, Egypt and Macedonia. He arranged carving of Buddhism's precepts on several rocks and pillars in India. These are noted as Ashoka's stone edicts. He lived for 62 years. India has adopted the Ashoka wheel and the lion's face as its national symbols. Ashoka is remembered in the world history for his outstanding qualities and noble character.

38. V. SHANTARAM

V.Shantaram was an extraordinary person in the Hindi film- world. He was also a pioneer of Indian films. Born on November 18, 1901 in Kolhapur, Vanakudre (near Bijapur) Shantaram began his career as an usher of screens at the drama company of Bal Gandharva (famous actor) in Kolhapur. Gradually, he gained ample experience in all sections of films.

Shantaram joined Baburao Painter, founder of the Maharashtra Film Company in Kolhapur, as an apprentice. Later, he established the Prabhat Film Company in Pune along with Damle and Fatelal. At the beginning of the 40s when the freedom movement gained momentum, he awakened the youth by producing many appropriate films with nationalistic thought. He became popular by producing films like Aadmi, Padosi, Duniya na Maane, and Sant Jnaneshwar under Prabhat symbol. Later, he moved to Bombay and established a studio called Rajkamal Kalamandir. He became a household name by making all-time-great films like Jeevan Yatra, Dr. Kotnis ki Amar Kahani, Do Aankhen Baarah Haath and Geet Gaya Paththarone under the symbol of Shantharam Films. Every film of his is a work of art. Jhanak Jhanak Paayal Baaje and Shakuntala films made by him attract connoisseurs even now. Shantaram, who ventured to reform society through films, had shown his patriotism. He had made Marathi films also like Pinjra. He was honoured with the Dada Saheb Phalke award. His autobiography, "Shantaram", has been published. His father was Raja and mother, Kamala. Later, he named his Rajkamal Kalamandir after them. For some time, he was President of the Children's Film Society also. His role as jailer in Do Aankhen Baarah Hath, which narrates human relationship between a jailer and prisoners, is unforgettable. He died on October 27, 1990 at the age of 90.

39. P.T.USHA

P.T.Usha is a well-known athlete who put India on the map of Olympics. She gained fame in athletics. She quit sport after the Asiad-1990 in Beijing.

Pilavulakandi Tekkaparambil Usha was born in 1964 in Kerala. At the age of 12 years, she joined a sports school at Cannanore and underwent training from O.M.Nambiar. An employee of Southern Railways, she became famous as an athlete through hard work. She is a good runner of Asia. She made a record at the Asiad-1986 by winning four gold and a silver medal. At the Asiad in Seoul, India won only five gold medals. Of them, four were bagged by Usha alone. At the Asiad 1982 also, she won gold medals in 100 and 200 metres running races. At the Olympics-1984 held in Los Angeles, though she missed narrowly, she was ranked fourth. She also made her presence felt at the Olympics-1988 in Seoul. She has done India proud as a competent runner.

40. PRAKASH PADUKONE

A world-renowned badminton player of India, Prakash Padukone was born on June 10, 1955 in Bangalore. He became a junior champion when he was just 14 years and a national champion on completing 15. He was the national champion of badminton for nine years (1970-1978). In 1980 he secured a Grandslam by winning three important international badminton tournaments. He represented India in Thomas Cup games. He won a bronze at the Asiad-1974 in Teheran and participated in the Commonwealth sports also. Prakash, who secured a place of pride for India in international badminton competitions, is a graduate. He is a successful player.

41. MIRZA GHALIB

Mirza Ghalib was a very great Urdu poet. Born in 1797 at Agra, his full name was Mirza Asadulla Beg Khan Ghalib. Born in a rich Muslim family, he lived in Delhi. He became a poet after learning Urdu and Persian. He lived luxuriously. His wedding with Umrao Begum was celebrated when he was just 13 years.

Ghalib's poems are combinations of very simple words. He is called the father of modern Urdu prose also. His prose too is equally splendid. Diwan-i-Ghalib in 10 volumes is a collection of his poems: It has been translated into several languages of the world and some languages of India. Full of romance, severe compassion and pain, they are popular with connoisseurs. Ghalib became famous in Arab countries as a Urdu and Persian poet. Nam-i-Ghalib, Latif-i-Gaibi, etc. are his notable works in prose. His Urdu-i-Hindi and Urdu-i-Mulla are collections of letters. He has duly depicted political and social conditions of his time.

Ghalib's final days were very horrible. Since he lived luxuriously as he liked in the beginning, at the end he suffered without financial strength. He died in 1869. His poems are popular even now.

42. RAJENDRA PRASAD

'Babu' Rajendra Prasad became the first President of Independent India by participating in the country's freedom struggle. Born on December 3, 1884 as a son of an Ayurvedic doctor, he obtained his M.A., degree in Calcutta. As worked as a lecturer at a college in Muzaffarpur for some time. As advised by his elder brother, he appeared for the law examination and passed in first class. He also earned a good name in the lawyer's profession. By virtue of his reputation, he worked as a professor for some time, in response to an invitation from Prof. Asutosh Mukherjee of the Calcutta University.

Influenced by Gandhiji who had returned to India after successfully launching satyagraha in South Africa, Rajendra Prasad also participated in India's freedom struggle. He gave up his legal profession. As a member of the Congress party, he worked as a leader in 1934, 1939 and 1947. He was president of the Congress session held in Bombay in 1934. Also, at the Tripura session in 1939 when Subhashchandra Bose resigned, he took over as President. Propagation of Hindi was a favourite subject to him. He also presided over the All India Hindi Literary Conference held in Nagpur. He was imprisoned during the freedom movement.

After advent of Independence in 1947, India became a Republic in 1950. Then Rajendra Prasad was elected as the first President of the country. He was a good writer also. He wrote about five books in Hindi and English. His book--Autobiography--won thousands of rupees as prize those days. He contributed it to a fund helping poor writers. His life abounded in sacrifice. Some of his lectures are published in the book, "Economics of Khadi".

Dr. Rajendra Prasad, who was saying that peace should prevail all over the world, lived loyally like King Janaka and Dharmaraya.

That great spirit set on March 1, 1963.

43. RAJA RAM MOHAN ROY

Born in 1772, Raja Ram Mohan Roy was a renowned social reformer of India. He tried and succeeded in eradicating the Sati system, Purda and wedding of children. He strove for education of women and remarriage of widows.

Raja Ram Mohan Roy firmly stood against all sorts

of social bigotry, conservatism and superstitions and advocated English and Western type of education for his countrymen. For these views, he was even expelled from his own family. He was a great scholar in Sanskrit too.

Roy made a wide study of different religions of the world, including Christianity and Islam. He was also proficient in many languages like, English, Persian, Arabic, Latin. French and even Hebrew. He was also a great scholar in Bangla and translated Vedas and Upanishads into this language.

Being born in an orthodox Brahmin family at Hoogly, Roy got into a job in the British East India Company in the year 1805. He retired from this service in the year 1815, and thereafter settled down at Calcutta, devoting himself to social service.

In the year 1830, he visited England to plead a case on behalf of the Moghul Emperor, who later honoured him with the title of 'Raja'.

Roy firmly believed in the fundamental unity of all religions. In the year 1814, he founded the 'Atmiya Samaj' and in the year 1828, the 'Brahmo Samaj'. Through these organisations, he wanted to expose the religious hypocrisies and check the growing influence of Christianity on Hindu religion and society.

The greatest achievement of Roy, however, was the

removal of the 'sati' system in Hindu society under which the wife jumped into the funeral pyre of her husband. It was due to the untiring efforts of Roy, that the then Governor-General of India, Lord William Bentinck abolished the system of 'sati' in the year 1829.

Roy is rightly called 'the father of Indian renaissance' or 'the father of Indian nationalism'. He breathed his last on 27th September, 1833, in England.

44. SARDAR VALLABHBHAI PATEL

Sardar Vallabhbhai Patel was well-known as the steel man of India. An Advocate, he was born in 1875 in a farmer's family. He participated in the freedom struggle, being influenced by Gandhiji's speeches. His role in Bardoli satyagraha was notable. His brother Vithalbhai Patel was also a freedom fighter. After India won freedom, he became the Deputy Prime Minister and succeeded in forging an integrated India by uniting over 500 princely states spread all over India. In spite of illness and imprisonment, he struggled hard to achieve his goal. He was responsible for reconstructing Somnath Temple in Gujarat. He died in 1950 due to severe illness.

45. LAL BAHADUR SHASTRI

Lal Bahadur Shastri, who succeeded Jawaharlal Nehru as the Prime Minister of India, managed the affairs of the nation, successfully. He was noted as a man of peace. He had participated in the freedom struggle and served in Nehru's cabinet. He faced Pakistan boldly when it invaded India in September, 1965. Though he participated successfully in the Indo-Pak agreement signed in Tashkent (U.S.S.R.), he passed away there itself on January 11, 1966. Only a few hours had elapsed after he signed the agreement.

Born in an ordinary middle-class family, on October 2, 1904 at Mughal Sarai in Uttar Pradesh, he spent his childhood in poverty and penury. But he was a man with humanism, honesty and straightforwardness. After education at Kashi Vidyapeeth, he devoted himself for social life and joined the 'Servants of People Society' founded by Lala Lajpat Rai.

That was the time when the freedom movement was at its peak. Shastri plunged into the freedom struggle. After India won Independence, his first entry was into U.P.political arena. Pandit Jawaharlal Nehru was much impressed with Shastri's ability and took him to the Centre-stage of Indian politics. He was made the general secretary of the Congress because of his organisational abilities.

Later, Lal Bahadur Shastri became the Union Minister for Railways. But he soon resigned from this post, owning moral responsibility for a major railway accident as the minister in charge of railway. He thus set a rare example and precedent in political administration.

When Jawaharlal Nehru died in the year 1964, he was elected as the third Prime Minister of India. His life was a saga of high moral conduct, simplicity of behaviour, sacrifice, politeness, and firm determination.

Lal Bahadur Shastri was posthumously conferred the 'Bharat Ratna', the highest civilian award, in recognition of his services to the nation. A memorial has been set up at Vijay Ghat, Delhi, which shall always remind us of his greatness.

Shastri impressed one and all by his statesmanship, honesty and administrative ability. He has left an indelible mark on the political scene of this country.

46. TENZING NORGAY

Born in a poor family of Nepal in 1914, Tenzing Norgay adopted Buddhism. He became an Indian citizen in 1933. Even from his childhood, mountaineering was a subject of interest to him. His name is written in golden letters in the history of mountaineering. He was a pioneer who climbed the Mount Everest (8,848 metres)--highest peak in the world. He embarked on the adventure of ascending the Himalayas as a member of the British mountaineering expedition led by John Hunt and reached the apex of the mountain on March 29, 1953. He attracted attention of the whole world.

In 1959, the Government of India honoured him with the Padma Bhushan award. Edmond Hillary of New Zealand was also with him. The Himalayan Mountaineering Institute was established in 1954 by the Government of West Bengal at Darjeeling for imparting training to mountaineers. Tenzing served as its first Director. He died in 1986.

47. SAROJINI NAIDU

Well-known as the "Nightingale of India", Sarojini Naidu was also a famous English poetess. She was an orator. She had participated in India's freedom struggle. She attended several sessions of the Congress. In 1925, she served as the President of the All India Congress Session. She was the first woman appointed as the Governor of Uttar Pradesh after India attained Independence. "Broken Wings" is her noted work.

48. JHANSI LAKSHMI BAI

The name of Queen Lakshmi Bai will be immortal in the history of India. The way she struggled against the British is legendary. She was born in Varanasi on November 16, 1834. Her name was Manikarnika. After the death of her mother, she went to Bithura along with her father. There she learnt horse riding and warfare. When she was just eight years, her wedding with Gangadhar Rao, the King of Jhansi was celebrated. Since then, she was known as the queen of Jhansi. In 1853, her only son and her husband died. The British Government did not allow her to adopt another as son.

In 1857, she died on the battle field fighting against the British in the first freedom struggle of India.

49. KAPIL DEV

Kapil Dev is the most famous cricketer of India. He was born on January 6, 1959 in Haryana. His father is a dealer in wood. Kapil Dev Nikhanji had not played cricket until he was 13. The family settled down in Chandigarh. Kapil Dev represented India as an all-rounder. After Ian Botham, it is Kapil who bagged 300 wickets and 3,000 runs in 83 matches. Credit for India's glorious win at the World Cup in England in 1983 goes to him.

Starting cricket in 1975, he figured in the team that visited Pakistan in 1978. He is also a noted bowler.

Kapil has partook in 131 test matches till now and scored a total of 5248 runs. His 163 runs in one-day match and 434 wickets in all, is a world record.

50. LALA LAJPAT RAI

Reputed as "The Lion of Punjab", Lala Lajpat Rai was born in 1865. He participated at the Congress session in Prayag in 1888. He plunged into the freedom struggle during his boyhood. He was exiled for six months in 1907. After familiarising with the condition of Indians, he visited England several times to discuss with the British. During World War I, he

went to America to hear their views on India's Independence. He established the Home Rule League there. He also launched "Young India", a monthly journal.

Lala Lajpat Rai did not believe--like Bal Gangadhar Tilak and Bipin Chandra Pal--that freedom can be gained by non-violence. These three heroes of Independence were well-known in the country then as Lal, Bal and Pal. Under the influence of Swami Dayananda, he established the Dayananda Anglo-Vedic College in Punjab. Lajpat Rai used to be always in the forefront of social service.

Lala Lajpat Rai was imprisoned for participating in the non-cooperation movement in 1920. He died due to the severe injuries he suffered in lathi charge by the police while waving black flags during the Simon Commission's visit to India. A great freedom lover, he was the author of renowned works, including "Self-Determination for India".

51. BHAGAT SINGH

Sardar Bhagat Singh was a brave freedom-fighter who became a martyr for India's Independence at the young age of 24 years. He was born on September 28, 1907 at Bangal village in Layalpur district of West Punjab.

Participation of his father and uncles in the freedom struggle and inspiration by his mother, Vidyavati, enhanced love for freedom in Bhagat Singh and prompted him also to fight. He plunged into Gandhiji's non-cooperation movement while still studying at school. He did not even marry and started working for "Pratap", a paper run by Ganesh Shankar Vidyarthi, a freedom lover. Just then, Chandrashekhar Azad, another revolutionary, befriended Bhagat Singh. Sukhdev and Raj Guru were his other friends. Together, they killed Sanders, a police officer, who was responsible for beating up Lajpat Rai to death.

Bhagat Singh was apprehended in the case of hurling a bomb during the Assembly session in 1929 and was sentenced to death. Bhagat Singh, Raj Guru and Sukh Dev were hanged on March 23, 1931. They breathed their last by kissing their nooses and chanting "Long live revolution". These three martyrs dedicated their lives for India's Independence. The nation will remember them for ever.

52. PREMCHAND

A renowned Hindi writer, Premchand, was born as Dhanpat Rai in 1880 at Varanasi in a poor family. India was waging the freedom struggle then. At that time, Dhanpat Rai Nawab wrote books in Urdu as "Raj". He wrote stories and novels in Hindi under the name Premchand.

Premchand is a very big name in Hindi literature.

His works, are shown as films and T.V. serials even now. Godaan, Kayakalp, Pratijnya, Nirmala, Seva Sadan, Premashram, Rangabhoomi and Karmabhoomi are his invaluable works. He was also publishing Hansa, a magazine. He was presented the title of Upanyaas Saamraat (King of novels). His works are noted for realistically depicting the life of the common man and his trials and tribulations. He wrote for about 30 years from 1901. His works usually project the life of the poor--perhaps because his own financial position was not good.

Premchand passed away in 1936.

53. KABIR

A great saint of the devotion (Bhakti) cult and a Muslim, Kabir became a devotee of Sri Rama and tried for equality of religions and castes. When differences of opinion occurred on the society's religion, he said that all religions are same and declared that there is only one God. There are many legends about Kabir. It is said that he was a weaver.

54. AUROBINDO

Born in the year 1872, Aurobindo was a philosopher and revolutionary of India. He is also known as a revolutionary- ascetic who propounded the theory of direct political action against the British rule, rather than moderate reformism. Ultimately, he ended as an ascetic. He is honoured in India for his nationalistic fervour, but the world admires him as a philosopher with divine vision.

Born in Calcutta, he tried to assimilate both Indian and Western philosophical thoughts and find the paths of divine communion and spiritual realization. He passed in the I.C.S. examination, but did not like to serve under the Britishers. He worked for some time with Sister Nivedita.

Aurobindo Ghosh participated in the freedom struggle of India. Later, he became a meditator and settled down in Pondicherry. He established an Ashram there. He was fond of seclusion. An eminent philosopher and poet, he wrote a huge book titled "Life Divine". His other works are: "Essays on Gita", "Basis of Yoga", "Love and Death" (Poem) and "Savitri" (Poetry).

The Aurobindo ashram at Pondicherry, attracts devotees from all over the world and is a center of meditation and a seat of studies on Aurobindo.

55. GOPALAKRISHNA GOKHALE

A famous statesman of India, Gopalakrishna Goknale dedicated himself to the freedom struggle and was a leader of the All India Congress. Gandhiji called him his 'Political Guru'(teacher). The Servants of India Society founded by him is rendering notable service even now.

Born in the year 1866 in a poor Maharashtrian Brahmin family, Gokhale lost his father when he was just 13 years of age. Even during his school days, he was known for his honesty, earnestness and sincerity. He graduated from Elphinestone College, Bombay. His excellent grasp of English language revealed itself very early and he became a good Parliamentarian in later years.

Gokhale's success as a teacher attracted the attention of great freedom fighters and educationists of those times, like Bal Gangadhar Tilak and Gopal Ganesh Agarkar. For sometime, he worked in the Fergusson College, where he had himself studied.

When he was just 20, he delivered his first speech on : "India under the British rule." This marked his first entry into the freedom struggle. He wrote articles in the English weekly "Mahratta" and in the year 1905, founded The Servants of India Society. He thus fulfilled his desire of spreading the work for the uplift of the poor. He was greatly influenced by Mahadev Govind Ranade, a great freedom fighter.

When Gandhiji returned to India from South Africa, he was too glad to have Gokhale as his 'political guru'. It was from Gokhale, that Gandhiji learnt the peaceful method of achieving swaraj. He joined the Indian National Congress in 1889 and spoke against the discrimination shown by the then British rulers towards Indians.

In 1905, he was elected President of the Congress session held at Varanasi. Gokhale firmly believed that swaraj could be achieved by peaceful means.

Exhaustion aggravated Gokhale's diabetes and

cardiac asthma. Two days before the end, with a firm hand, he completed a draft scheme of constitutional reforms on the request of Lord Willingdon, Governor of Bombay state.

On February 19, 1915, the end came to Gokhale peacefully. The great leader was no more.

While the whole nation mourned his death, Gandhiji in a tribute said: "I was in quest of a really truthful hero in India and I found him in Gokhale. His love and reverence for India were truly genuine. For serving his country, he completely eschewed all happiness and self-interest."

56. NARAYANA GURU

A great saint, born in Kerala, Narayana Guru was influential after Adi Shankaracharya. He lived in the early years of the 20th century and strove to remove untouchability. He opposed the caste system.

57. J.R.D.TATA

Jehangir Ratanji Dadabhai Tata who is described as the father- figure of Indian industry, hails from the renowned Tata family. The Tatas belong to the Parsi community. They first settled down in Navsari, a village near Bombay, in 1142 AD.

J.R.D.Tata, who shone as the brighest star in this family, was born on the 29th, July 1904 in Paris. His father was an Indian Parsi, Ratanji Tata and mother Sujaine, a French lady. He recieved his primary

education both in Paris and Bombay. Although he wanted to pursue his studies in Cambridge, he did not do so.

Tata was inspired right from his childhood to become an adventurous pilot, by Louis Blerio who was the first to cross the English channel by an airplane. He also worked in the French army for sometime, but was called back to India by his father to work for the Tata group of companies. He joined the Bombay flying club and became the first Indian to obtain a pilot licence.

In the year 1932, Tata introduced in India the use of airplanes for transporting goods and postal articles. In the year 1982, Tata re-enacted his maiden flight from Bombay to Karachi in his own plane. He started the Tata airlines which later became the Air India. He developed the Tata group of industries and supported the freedom struggle.

Tata set up a large group of industries in India that touched almost all spheres of human activity. He became a model employer and gave employment to lakhs of Indians, so much so that today he is a house-hold name in India.

Tata set up such wide ranging industries, companies and organisations in India like, airplanes, textiles, tea, locomotives, electrics, transport, detergents, scientific establishments, social service organisations, and even common salt.

In recognition of his services in the various fields of human activity, he was awarded many national and international awards. Among the Indian awards were: Padma Vibhushana in the year 1955, and the highest civilian honour, the Bharath Ratna in the year 1992.

Tata breathed his last on November 29, 1993 at Geneva, Switzerland. The whole world mourned his death.

58. CHANAKYA

Chanakya is a legendary and historical name in India. The name 'Chanakya' is associated with shrewdness, statesmanship and the art of political administration.

Chanakya, the greatest of the diplomats in the world of olden era, is supposed to have been living around 300 BC. He was a sage-like person who, by his political shrewdness and politics of expediency, founded the mighty Mauryan empire in India. He was an expert in economics, diplomacy and political administration. He was well-read, determined in his policies and principles and foresighted.

Legend has it that once he was invited to the court of Nanda king and suffered an insult there. Chanakya took a vow to bring down the Nanda dynasty. With the help of a brave and capable general, Chandragupta, he succeeded in fulfilling his ambition, and founded the Mauryan dynasty in Magadh.

Again, with the help of Chandragupta Maurya, he expelled the Greek invaders from India. Chanakya was a friend, guide and philosopher to Chandragupta Maurya. He is also believed to be the author of the book "Artha sastra", the classical Indian treatise on the art of administration and economics. It lays down the rules of governance and gives a detailed account of the state of affairs at that time.

Chanakya was born in a poor Brahmin family of Taxila. His real name was Vishnugupta. Chanakya is also known as 'Kautilya' because of his 'kutila neeti' or the cunning art of diplomacy.

In his personal life, Chanakya was said to be a self-less person who only worked for the welfare of the king, kingdom and the people. He lived an ascetic life even though he was very near and dear to the king in those times and could have enjoyed the luxury and comforts of royal life. He actually lived in a mud house near the king's place. A very famous Sanskrit play, "Mudra Rakshasa", has for its theme one of the diplomatic feats of Chanakya.

According to legend, Chanakya told Chandra Gupta that the weed or unwanted grass must not be just cut at the ground level and thrown out, but must be pulled out along with its root so that it may not grow again. Just like this act, an enemy must be defeated and destroyed in full so that he may not raise his head again. This was 'Chanakya-neeti'. However, a person is now called a 'Chanakya', not only if he is wise and shrewd, but also if he is wily and cunning in his ways.

59. RAM MANOHAR LOHIA

Ram Manohar Lohia was an undaunted brave son of India. He was the uncrowned king of millions of Indian minds and hearts. He was, like Dr. Ambedkar at a later date, the champion of the poor, weak and oppressed masses of India. Even with such an image, he held no political power or authority.

Lohia was born on March 23, 1910 in a village, Akbarpur, in Faizabad district, Uttar Pradesh. His father, Hira Lal, was a teacher by profession and his mother, Chanda. Ram was their only child. Ram's family business was in iron or 'Loha' in Hindi and hence he acquired 'Lohia' to his name.

In 1921, the young, Ram met Jawaharlal Nehru. He had earlier been attracted to Gandhiji's ideals and had joined the civil disobedience movement. In spite of his criticism of Nehru when he became a Parliamentarian later, he was a great admirer of Nehru.

After passing his matric examination in 1925 with distinction, Ram studied at the Banaras Hindu University college. He developed into a brilliant scholar and a fiery orator. Later, he did his B.A., from Calcutta University. He became a student- leader and joined the freedom movement. He also met Subhash-chandra Bose.

Later, he went to Germany for higher studies and refused to go to London for studies because he hated the British who had subjugated India. Soon, he was known to be a revolutionary and a rebel against the British empire. He returned to India in 1933 after obtaining his Ph.D., in Berlin University, with his chosen subject of 'salt satyagraha' as thesis. He then joined the Indian National Congress.

In the year 1934, some enthusiastic persons like Jayakprakash, Ashok Mehta, Yusuf Meherally and Achyut Patwardhan, formed a new group and named it Congress Socialist Party.

The then British government, arrested Lohia on June 7, 1940 and imprisoned him. He was humiliated and even tortured there. He was released in December, 1941 along with other leaders. He participated in the 'Quit India' movement in 1942. Lohia went underground and spent time in dense forests and in Nepal and helped the freedom fighters and even set up the 'Congress Radio' to pass on secret messages to the freedom-fighters. He was again arrestsesd in May, 1944 in Bombay. He was put in Lahore jail in solitary confinement. No words can describe the agony he suffered there.

Gandhiji had told Lohia that he would like to tell him something important. But it never materialised because Gandhiji fell to an assassin's bullet, suddenly.

Lohia's role in Independent India was unique. His 'garibi hatao' (removal of poverty) slogan was adopted by Indira Gandhi at a later date, though not in the same sense.

Lohia remained a bachelor throughout his life. On

September 30, 1967, he was operated upon in New Delhi for a simple ailment, but later complications arose and his health deteriorated; he was in a critical state.

Lohia's end came on October 12, 1967. He left no property, no bank balance-- only millions of admirers and his ideas of socialism.

60. HARGOBIND KHORANA

Dr. Hargobind Khorana is an Indian-born American scientist. Born in India in the year 1922, he went to United States for higher studies in genetics.

He shared the 1968 Nobel Prize in Physiology or Medicine with Robert W.Holley and Marshall W.Nirenberg for interpretation of the genetic code and its function in protein synthesis. Khorana helped to decipher the genetic code by synthetically recreating each of the 64 possible triplets of DNA (Deoxyribo Nucleic Acid) nucleotides .

DNA is a biological self-replicating macro-molecule which plays a vital role in heredity. It is packed in chromosomes. It is the chief material in chromosomes, the cellular components that govern the heredity of an animal or plant. The DNA in chromosomes furnishes the 'daughter cells' with a complete set of instructions for the cells, own development and the growth of its descendants. DNA is made up of phosphate, a kind of sugar, and compounds called 'bases'. Life's messages coded in the DNA are decoded by a series of mechanism which involve transcription and translation to produce proteins. These messages are passed down to generations by a process of replication.

Thanks to Hargobind Khorana's efforts, scientists can now at will, cut and join DNA, through genetic engineering. He was able to synthesise the first wholly-artificial gene. That gene was called 'Escherichia coli'.

DNA finger-printing is now developed, which helps in establishing lineages and for identifying criminals, as the DNA is unique to any individual.

The above scientific and technological developments go to show the key role played by Dr. Hargobind Khorana, the Indian- born American scientist. In fact, if only Dr. Khorana's genius was not allowed to go abroad, he would have been a great asset for the scientific and biological development of this great motherland of ours.

It may also be mentioned here that chromosomes 'x' and 'y' are the determining factors of sex --male or female--at the embryo stage.

61. V.S.SRINIVASA SASTRI

V.S.Srinivasa Sastri, who later came to be known to the world as the 'Silver-tongued Right Honourable Srinivasa Sastri', was born on September 22, 1869, in a village called Valangaiman near Kumbakonam, Tamil Nadu.

Sastri's father was a priest by profession. He was unable to bring up his seven children with his meagre income. His mother was a very pious lady. Sastri was brought up in a religious, tradition-bound way. He was taught puranic methods and traditional way of life and literature.

Sastri passed his matriculation in 1884 at the age of 15. His father had no means to send him to a college. Fortunately for him, being merited, he could get entry into a college without paying fees. Sastri came out of the college with high merit. Later, he was throughout a rank holder in Madras state.

Sastri started his career as a teacher and soon became an excellent master. At the age of 26, he became the vice-principal of a municipal college at Salem. He soon involved himself in public affairs and came into contact with some great freedom fighters of those days. Sastri was inspired by the ideals of Gopalakrishna Gokhale and was also engagaed in writing articles in journals and newspapers. In February 1906, Sastri met Gokhale who was considered the 'political guru' of Gandhiji. He soon became a member of the Servants of India Society started by Gokhale.

When Gokhale died, Sastri was made President of the Servants of India Society. He now devoted himself wholly to politics and attained a unique distinction. Sastri, a teacher, became Sastri, a statesman.

Sastri had got married at the age of 14 while still a school-boy. His wife, Parvati, was much younger. In the year 1896, Parvati died, leaving a child. Sastri married again the following year. Lakshmi, his second wife, proved to be a great moral supporter to him. Sastri went to South Africa in 1927 as the agent of the Government then. He returned from South Africa in 1928 and was conferred the honour of Knighthood. (K.C.I.E- Knight Commander of the Indian Empire), but he declined it, remembering how his guru, Gokhale, had turned down a similar offer.

In the year 1913, he was nominated as a member of the legislative council, Madras. He proved his merit as a legislator also. His eloquence, courage and persistance impressed one and all. Between the years 1921 and 1932, Sastri was frequently deputed overseas on official and non-official missions, mostly relating to problems of Indians living abroad. He was invited by the heads of many countries for discussions. Every where, he espoused the cause of India and Indians.

In his very last letter from his death-bed to Gandhiji, pleading with him not to accept the idea of Pakistan, Sastri said: "The Punjab and Bengal would be ruined, and blast your memory if you gave them up. Do not let any part of India go out and become independent. It is bound to be a lasting enemy and blistering sore to India."

How prophetic!

Early in 1946, Sastri fell ill and was admitted to

the General Hospital, Madras. During this time, Gandhiji visited him thrice. Sastri was overwhelmed and in a mood of affection and reverence, spoke to Gandhiji comparing him now and then with Lord Rama, as Gandhiji kept protesting tenderly: "What nonsense, Sastri".

In a tribute to Sastri when he passed away on April 17, 1946, Sarojini Naidu said: "Next to Rabindranath Tagore, Sastri was the greatest ambassador and interpreter of Indian culture abroad."

PART II

1. WILLIAM SHAKESPEARE

Every work of William Shakespeare, a great poet and playwright, is spectacular. His works are being reviewed even now. His talent was exceptional. He is a very big name in the world of literature.

Shakespeare was born on April 23, 1564 at Stratford, on the banks of river Avon. Starting as a poet at the age of 18, he dazzled as a very big playwright. At the same age, he married Anne Hathaway, who was older than him by eight years! He had begun to live independently. In addition to his profession, he acted at a theatre in London. He used to appear on the stage till 1611. Later, he returned to Stratford and died there in 1616.

Shakespeare's creation of literature is considered wonderful. Both English literature and world literature are incomplete without his writings. He has written over 30 plays and some sonnets. Some are tragedies, some comedies and melodramas.

His first work was a lengthy poem. It is titled Venus and Adonis. It was published in 1593 and became popular. Romeo and Juliet, Julius Caesar, Othello, Macbeth, King Lear and Hamlet are famous tragedy plays. As You Like It, Midsummer Night's Dream, The Taming of the Shrew, The Merchant of Venice are some well-known comedy plays. In all these plays, he has created several interesting characters. Each character is diverse. These plays are liked even now. Hamlet is considered as his most outstanding work.

A quotable quote from Shakespeare about the meaning of life runs thus: " Life is a tale, told by an ediot, full of sound and fury, signifying nothing."

2. CHARLES DICKENS

A world-famous novelist, Charles Dickens, was born in 1812 in a poor family of England. In his childhood, he suffered financially. His father was an ordinary clerk. After growing up, he worked at a law office for some time. He was reading literature during leisure time and also learnt shorthand. He was a reporter at Parliament. He contributed several articles to a paper under the title Pickwick Papers from 1837 to 1839. This earned him fame. He was recognised as a superb novelist. He had an extraordinary command over English. His novels depict the lives of different strata of society in general and the poor and the exploited, in particular. Oliver Twist, David Copperfield, Pickwick Papers, Great Expectations, A Tale of Two Cities are some of his renowned works. It was Dickens who created several memorable characters after Shakespeare. Humour and wisecracks which refresh the mind. are unique features of Dickens' works.

Charles John Hafam Dickens died in 1870 at the age of 58. Depiction of labourers and poor people in his works was perhaps the result of the difficulties he suffered in childhood.

3. ABRAHAM LINCOLN

Abraham Lincoln was perhaps the pioneer who strove to eradicate slavery in the world. He was born on February 12, 1809 in a poor family at Kentucky, United States of America. Thomas Lincoln was his father.

Abraham Lincoln had to experience much difficulties in his childhood. Though he was intelligent, he could not study much due to financial problems. Beginning his career as a clerk in a shop, he later studied law and became a lawyer. In 1847, he was elected to the American Congress and in 1861, he even became the President of the United States of America. He strove to uphold unity and integrity of the country. During the civil war of 1863, he successfully eradicated slavery in the United States. His greatest achievements were, becoming the President of America and striving all his life to abolish slavery. The southern states of America were agriculture-oriented; they wanted slavery to be retained for their economic prosperity. But the northern states were industrialised. Having achieved economic self- reliance, they encouraged abolition of slavery. Just then, civil war broke out. Lincoln felt that a civil war was needed for the country's federation and abolition of slavery. Determination and adventurism of completing the mission were the hallmarks of his success.

He was assassinated by a mad actor while watching a drama along with his wife in Washington. Americans for ever recall his sacrifice and adventure.

4. LEO TOLSTOY

Leo Tolstoy inspired the idea of non-cooperation in Mahatma Gandhi. Gandhiji's principles of truth and non-violence almost resemble the principles of morality and spirituality, etc. taught by Tolstoy. He influenced Gandhiji's life tremendously. He was a renowned novelist of Russia. He also wrote stories for children. "War and Peace" is his well-known work. This novel has the background of Napolean who invaded Russia in 1812; it depicts the Russians' reaction and aspirations. This work also depicts the theoretical and moral basis of the war. Tolstoy was also an outstanding social thinker. He said that God's existence should be believed for cleansing one's soul. Anna Karenina, Teachings of Christ, Resurrection, Wisdom of Children, etc., are some of his other works. Born in 1828, he has written his autobiography also. He denounced the way Britishers treated Indians. He died in 1910.

5. FOOT BALL KING PELE

Pele is the greatest of the football players of the world so far. Edson Arrentice Donyaciments or Pele is like another name for football. He was born on October 23, 1940 in a poor Negro family of Brazil.

Pele played his first football match in 1959 as a member of the Santos Club team. He scored his first goal in that match. Since then, he has never given up the coveted position of the world's greatest football player. He has scored 1,281 goals in 1,363 first class matches played by him. He joined the national football team of Brazil at the age of 16. He won his 1,000th goal while playing his 909th first class match in 1969. He married Rose Mary Dose in 1966.

The Brazilian football team won international matches under the leadership of Pele. In recognition of his services to football, he was awarded several national and international honours. Postage stamps were released in his honour. He was honoured by Marshal Tito, President of Yugoslavia. He was also honoured as a 'Black Diamond'. He was admired by two lakh sports lovers when he played against Yugoslavia at Markana stadium of Rio de Janerio on July 18, 1971. He bade good-bye to football there and retired.

In 1970, Pele was honoured with a gold medal for his win at the World Cup Soccer.

"Pele always loves perfection. He never likes to disappoint his admirers", says Julio Macio, his close friend and coach. Globo TV of Brazil has been making a TV film on Pele. He was also honoured by his favourite Santos Soccer Club on completing 21 years as a football player. He is a symbol of Brazil's prestige. Pele's name is associated with football. Though retired, he has not lost enthusiasm in the play.

6. LEO HENDRICK BAKELAND

We see plastic in one form or the other now when we look around anywhere on earth, be it a snow-clad mountain or a deserted hill- top. Though natural products are the source of plastic, it is fully synthetic. Plastic was first produced as Bakelite in 1907 by Leo Hendrick Bakeland (1863-1944), an American scientist. He was born at Ghent in Belgium. When he was just eight years of age, his school teacher had told him the story of Benjamin Franklin, the first scientist of America. Bakeland had never dreamt that he would become an American citizen. His only interest was science. He studied at the Ghent University and secured his doctorate degree at the age of 21 years. He obtained a scholarship and went to the United States of America. Thanks to the scholarship, he gained vast knowledge by visiting universities in Germany, France, Scotland and England. When he was in New York, by virtue of his photography as a hobby, he secured a job at H.T. Anthony & Company. There, Bakeland opened his own laboratory. He conducted research and made special photographic paper which could be clear in artificial light. Till then, photographers were clicking in sunlight. Photography was not possible without sunlight. Then, Bakeland produced vela paper. Some people opposed its use initially. But later, they welcomed it when it was manufactured on a large scale.

Bakeland later aimed at making a resin which was resistant to oils and acid. Once he mixed Formaldehyde and Carbolic acid. He guessed that a product like lac may be obtained by dissolving the solution obtained by such a mixture. The result secured with such a liquid was water-resistant, hard and a bad conductor of electricity. It was hard after drying and could not be dissolved again. Bakeland put the mix in a glass vessel and boiled it at a higher temperature. The mix liquefied and in a little time, turned transparent like glass and took the shape of the vessel. When the vessel was cooled, a vessel-shaped glass-like container fell down.

Bakeland was happy about his achievement. The first plastic container of the world was produced.

This was the first attempt at thermo-setting plastics. It hardens after boiling. Its shape does not change after cooling. Bakeland announced the discovery of such a product around 1909 and called that light commodity as bakelite. Since bakelite was a bad conductor of electricity, it very much attracted the manufacturers of electrical appliances. Bakelite replaced celluloid material which were known to liquefy on heating. Bakelite is used now in the manufacture of pens, electric switches, telephones, radio parts, cigarette holders, etc.,

Thanks to bakelite, Bakeland acquired both wealth and recognition at his old age. In 1924, he was elected president of the American Chemical Society. He died at Beacon near New York in 1944. The world shall not forget this scientist, who was known for his perseverance and restraint, and very much responsible for the various forms of plastic which constitutes 80% of modern man's daily utilities, excelling even iron and steel.

7. NELSON MANDELA

Dr. Nelson Mandela, the only hope of South Africans and President of the African National Congress, was released in February 1990 after imprisonment for a long period of 27 years for fighting for the rights of Blacks.

Nelson Mandela was born in a rich family on July 18, 1918. He secured a job at a firm in Johannesburg in 1942 at the age of 24. On the very first day of his service, a White typist called him and said: "When the boy brings tea today, take your share of tea from the tray. We have procured two new cups for you and Gaul Radicke. You should use only those tumblers". This instigated him to struggle for long. On another occasion, a lady typist treated Nelson as her subordinate. All this because he was a Black.

Bitterness of the apartheid grieved Nelson. He rebelled against disrespect and violence to Blacks by the White minority and declared a struggle. He was imprisoned due to his continuous struggle. Mandela, who spent more than a quarter of a century in jail, has immense respect for Mahatma Gandhi. While in prison, he read books on Gandhiji and his struggle for Independence. But he did not hate the Whites who put him in jail. On July 17,1988 he celebrated his 70th birthday in prison.

Nelson is a good writer. He has written an autobiography titled "The struggle of my life". Several international honours have been conferred on him for crusading against racial discrimination. When he was released in February 1990, F.W.De Clerk, President of South Africa, helped him. Mandela is also an orator. He practised law for some time.

In October 1990, the Government of India honoured him by presenting the "Bharat Ratna" award, the highest civilian honour conferred by it. Mandela said on that occasion: "I have come to India to strengthen the mutual commitment to the struggle which would continue till success is achieved". He was presented the Jamnalal Bajaj award also. In response, he stated: "this is a befitting honour to the South African people who are struggling for freedom on the strength of Gandhiji's principles".

The release of Nelson Mandela has infused much strength to the struggle of South Africa's Blacks.

In the general elections held in May 94, Dr. Mandela was elected President of South Africa in a smooth and democratic transfer of power from his predecessor, De Clerk. Mahatma Gandhi's dream of Independence for South Africa thus became a reality nearly a century after his struggle there.

8. AGATHA CHRISTIE

Agatha Christie is one of the most popular writers of the world. She was born on September 15, 1890 at Tarquary, on the sea coast of England's south-eastern province. Fredrick Miller was her father and Clara, her mother. Her father was interested in amateur dramas. After his death, the mother and daughter migrated to Cairo, capital of Egypt, on medical advice. Agatha used to read novels from her childhood. She participated in many dance programmes at Cairo. She was 20 years then.

On returning to Britain, Agatha started writing stories and poems. She married Archie, who had secured a Colonel's post by representing France in World War I.

Agatha has written 78 detective novels and 19 plays. Non-stop show of her play, "The Mouse trap", in the open theatre of London for 30 years is a record. By 1970's, she was renowned as the queen of detective story writers. She also served as a nurse for some time. In 1928, she obtained a divorce from Archie. At the age of 40, she married Max Mellovan, who was 15 years younger to her.

It is almost impossible to say how many copies of Agatha Christie's books are sold till now. As per an estimate, one billion copies in 63 foreign languages and one billion in English have been sold. Cinemas and TV serials based on her novels have also been made.

Her popularity can be known by the fact that works of no writer except Shakespeare, are sold in such a huge number as those of Christie. The Guiness Book of Records carries her name as the most successful of all novelists.

She died at the age of 85 in 1976.

9. THOMAS ALVA EDISON

Edison was born in a poor family of America in 1847. He had no means even to study. However, he always used to conduct some experiment. He worked as a telegraph operator after searching for a job throughout the country. He saved some money from his earnings and opened a workshop, where he conducted hundreds of experiments. He invented several machines. Some of his inventions are gramaphone (phonograph), projector, electric bulb, voice recorder, telegraph printer, and transmitter. Edison, who used to say that "his work was making people happy", is a very great scientist of the 20th century. During World War I, he worked for the American Government. He secured a medal on that occasion for about 40 odd inventions he achieved. He researched continuously and invented several techniques.

Edison passed away on October 18, 1931.

10. DALAI LAMA

Tibetan mountains are full of gorges. It is also called the heart of Asia. Its citizens consider Dalai Lama as their god. Dalai means ocean of knowledge. Dalai Lama, religious head of Tibetans is also called King. The rulers of Tibet since the 17th century were known Dalai Lamas.

The present Dalai Lama was installed in 1935. He was just two years of age then. His coronation was celebrated in 1940. He assumed power after undergoing training till 1950. Herare of Austria imparted modern education to him. Dalai Lama began to use modern instruments and love science. When the Chinese invaded independent Tibet, he fled to India. In 1989, he was awarded the Nobel prize for fighting for the freedom of Tibetans from the Chinese rule.

11. GARY SOBERS

Garyfield Sobers was born on July 28, 1936 at Bridgetown, Capital of Barbados (West Indies). He played cricket from his childhood and became famous when he was just 16. Well-known as a left hand cricketer, he has scored over 8,000 runs in 93 test matches. His speciality lies in his century of catches. An all- rounder in cricket, he is now imparting training to young cricketers after his retirement. He made a record by scoring 36 runs in a single over on August 31, 1948.

He batted 26 centuries in his test life.

The Government of Barbados has released a postage stamp in honour of Sir Garyfield Sobers. He was the captain of the West Indies team in 1963.

12. CHARLIE CHAPLIN

Charlie Chaplin is a world-famous humourous actor. He made spectators not only laugh endlessly but also think.

Chaplin was born on April 16, 1889 at Kennystun, London. Since he became an orphan in his childhood, he had to look for a job. So he could not study much. At the age of 15, he acted along with his brother in a humorous play. As his acting was liked by people, Chaplin made acting his profession. In 1910, he went to America along with a drama troupe. Maxet provided an opportunity to Chaplin to act in his film. In 1914, the first film in which Chaplin acted, was released. "Modern Times," "The Great Dictator," and "Limelight", are some of the films in which he acted.

Chaplin, by his acting, has dazzled as a renowned comedian. When a film was made mocking Hitler's dictatorship during World War II (1939-1945), Chaplin's role in it as Hitler was acclaimed. In this film, called "The Great Dictator," he acted as a barber also. Comedian Chaplin died at the age of 88.

13. GEORGE BERNARD SHAW

George Bernard Shaw was a world-famous British playwright after William Shakespeare. He was known by the acronym of G.B.S.

Shaw was born on July 26, 1856 in Dublin, Ireland. He had his early education in Dublin. After school education, he worked in an office as a clerk and treasurer till 1876. Literature was his abiding interest. He started writing novels to become a writer. But he did not succeed in that "stream" of literature. So he began to write plays. "Widowers' Houses" was his first successful play, written in 1892. In this play, he has expressed his views on the problem of London's slums.

He continued to write plays till "The Apple Cart" in 1929. He was awarded the Nobel prize for literature for his play, "St. Joan", in 1925. "Man and Superman" "Arms and the Man", "The Doctor's Dilemma", "Back to Methuselah" are some of his other plays. He wrote and published five novels from 1879 to 1883. Two of his famous novels are "Love Among the Artists" and "Cashel Byron's Profession".

Shaw has written a total of 50 plays. Sharp writing and a tinge of humour are the hallmarks of his works. Through his plays, he discusses current politics, social and religious problems. As a result, he was known as a social reformer also. He was well-known as a writer even before he received the Nobel prize. He is also known as a good critic, who led a simple life. He was a vegetarian, teetotaller and non-smoker.

Shaw passed away at the age of 94 years in 1950.

His quotable quote is: "life is not a little candle; it is a flashing torch".

14. KHAN ABDUL GAFFAR KHAN

Khan Abdul Gaffar Khan, who was admired as the "Frontier Gandhi", was one of the great followers of Gandhiji. He was a freedom fighter also. Born in a rich family of the North-West Frontier Province (NWFP) of India, he could take firm decisions from his boyhood. Mild natured, he called himself a soldier of the freedom struggle. He opposed the British even when he was young. He not only organised people of the NWFP, but also remained committed to Gandhiji's principles. NWFP was not yet divided then. His aspiration and struggle for freedom of the Pathans or Pakhtoons continued even after India's division and merger of the NWFP in Pakistan.

During the British rule, he was imprisoned for the first time for three years. After his release, he launched the Khudai Khimatgar organisation and inducted Pathans in the freedom movement. The Muslim League did not support him. But the

Congress extended support. He became a Congressman. His followers used to call him Badshah Khan. The people of India had a special respect for him.

In 1969, he came from Afghanistan in response to an invitation from the Indian Government on a lecture tour. In 1985, he participated in the historical centenary of the Congress celebrated in Bombay. He was over 90 years old then. He died a few years later. In 1987, the Government of India conferred the Bharat Ratna award on him. He was the first foreign dignitary to receive the award.

15. MARTIN LUTHER KING

Martin Luther King who became a martyr when he was felled by a bullet, was known as "Gandhi of Negros".

Born on January 15, 1929 at Atlanta (Georgia), he studied philosophy in Boston University. He secured a job at a church. Works of the American writer Thoreau influenced him very much. He resolved to fight for the civil rights of Negros in the USA and followed the path of non-violence like Gandhiji. But the Black leaders themselves did not support him. Supporters of racialism did not like his move to involve people of all races in his struggles.

King continued his struggle for equal civil rights for Negros in the United States of America. As a result, American Negros could secure due rights on the basis of equality. Even the White race appreciated his efforts. He conducted his peaceful movement by establishing the Southern Christian Leadership Conference. When he visited India in 1959, he said that the principles of Mahatma Gandhi and Nehru should be followed for peace all over the world.

King breathed his last as a victim to the bullet of a White man at Memphis, Tennessee, in 1968. He was granted the Nobel Peace Prize in 1964. The Government of India honoured him by presenting the Jawaharlal Nehru award for international peace. The entire world mourned the death of King, who was also known as the "American Gandhi".

16. ALBERT EINSTEIN

One of the great scientists of the 20th century, Albert Einstein was born on March 14th 1879 at Ulma, Germany, in a Jewish family. In 1894, he became a citizen of Switzerland and completed his early education there. He studied for four years at the Polytechnical Academy, Zurich. He became a graduate in 1900 and obtained his Ph.D. from the Zurich University in 1905. In 1912, he became a professor at the Zurich polytechnic. In 1914, he was invited to become a professor in the Prussian Academy of Science at Berlin. When Adolph Hitler, who hated Jews, assumed power in 1933, he quit Germany and settled down in America permanently.

By 1919, Einstein had gained international recognition as a great scientist. His scientific inventions were lauded by the Royal Society of London. Thereafter, he started explaining his scientific achievements to intellectuals by touring the entire Europe. In 1921, he was awarded the Nobel Prize for Physics. A paper presented by him on relativity brought about a revolution in the world of science. The speed of light will be the same, whether a thing is moving towards light or away from it, states the theory of relativity. This theory of his shed new light on space, time and heaviness.

Einstein passed away on April 18, 1955 at the age of 76 at Princeton. His scientific achievements are remarkable.

17. BOBBY FISCHER

Bobby Fischer is called the "King of chess." Born on March 9, 1943 at Chicago, his full name is James Robert Fischer. He did not study further after he evinced interest in chess while studying at the high school in New York. He devoted all his time to reading books and magazines on chess. He became the national chess champion of the United States of America at the age of 13. He created a record by winning over Boris Spasky of earlier Russia in 1972. Spasky was the world chess champion till then. After this success, Americans called Fischer the King of chess. Gary Kasparov of Russia was another famous chess player like him.

18. LUSHUN

Lushun was a renowned writer of China. He was born on September 25, 1881 at Shaoshing. At the age of 18, he went to Nanking for studies. In 1902, he proceeded to Japan and joined a college there to study medicine. But he returned to Tokyo without completing the course. After returning to China from Japan in 1908, he aroused Chinese youths by his revolutionary activities. With writing as his medium, he indulged in political activities also. It is interesting to know that he fought against the Japanese who invaded China in 1930.

"People's writer", Lushun, struggled for the social rights of his people. He not only worked for the prosperity of the society's weaker and exploited people, but also tried to eradicate the deep-rooted superstitions among the people. 'Diary of a Mad Man','Warm Air','My Old House' and 'Worship of the New Year', are his famous literary works.

Lushun died on October 19, 1936.

19. WILHELM K. ROENTGEN

Wilhelm K. Roentgen was Germany's physicist and Nobel scientist. He was born in 1845 as the son of a farmer, and had his early education in Switzerland and Holland. He obtained his doctorate in physics from the Zurich University and undertook several research projects. He is noted as the scientist who invented X-ray. This was accidentally detected in 1895.

One day, Roentgen was conducting research with a cathode ray tube. He observed rays "which were invisible" and different from cathode rays, when cathode rays hit either walls of the tube or an element of higher atomic weight. He detected that these rays could pass through different things. Since he could not understand the nature of these rays, he called them X-rays. Later, these rays became a big boon to medical field and physics. Soon X-rays were used in British hospitals and helped to treat physical injuries. Roentgen's contribution to the world of science is of great importance. He conducted experiments even to know the influence of electricity on crystals.

Roentgen received the Nobel Prize in 1901. He was the first to get it in physics. He died in 1923 in Munich. Now, everyone knows about X-rays.

20. YURI GAGARIN

Yuri Gagarin was a Russian astronaut. He was also the first astronaut of the world. He passed through space in Vostok-1 launched on April 12, 1961 and returned safely.

Gagarin spent a total of 108 minutes in space, at an altitude of 340 km from the earth, and at a staggering speed of 28,090 km per hour. He made a voyage round the earth that took him 89.34 minutes.

Since then, Gagarin is known to be not only the first space traveller, but also, the first person to fly at such a great height.

Gagarin was born in a remote Russian village. He was just 27 years of age when he went into the orbit. The successful space flight by Gagarin not only generataed much excitement throughout the world, but it also opened up a new era in space science--the era of manned space flight.

This brave hero of space died in an air accident on March 27, 1968 at the age of just 34 years.

He was honoured with the 'Order of Lenin', 'Gold Star Medal' and the 'Hero of the Soviet Union'.

21. ALEXANDER

Alexander was the son of King Phillip II of Macedonia. He was an adventurist and an astute aspirant. After his father's death, he became the king of Macedonia at the age of 20 in 336 B.C. After establishing his rule in Greece, he aspired to win the entire world and control it. He formed a huge army for this purpose and gathered weapons.

In 334 B.C. he started his victory march towards the East. Passing through the Asia Minor, the Mediterranean border area and Phinisia, he reached the Nile river valley. He annexed Egypt and established Alexandria city in 332 B.C. He named it after himself to commemorate his victory. After annexing Persia, he invaded India by passing through the Hindukush. In 326 B.C. he camped on the banks of the Sindhu river. Ambi the ruler of Takshashila, welcomed him and compromised with him. Both became friends. But Puroorava, who cherished freedom, ably faced Alexander. Puroorava was ruling his state situated between the Jheelum and the Chinab rivers. Both waged a fierce war. Though Puroorava fought bravely against Alexander, he lost due to rain. But Alexander, who was impressed with his capability and love for independence, returned the state won by him.

In 326 B.C. Alexander crossed the Ravi river and successfully annexed all areas to its east. Although he aspired to subject the Magadh kingdom under his control, he returned to Greece, since his army wanted to go back. He died in Babylon at the age of 33 years.

Alexander is a significant personality in world history.

22. DONALD BRADMAN

Perhaps no other game has attracted sports lovers of the world as much as cricket.

Donald Bradman is the greatest cricketer of the world. He was born on August 27, 1908 in New South Wales, Australia. He was recognised as a good batsman from his early years. Centuries scored by him in later life are innumerable! He was selected to play in a test match for the first time in 1928. The greatest batsman of the world now, he scored 5,996 runs in 52 test matches. He scored 99.94 runs in an innings on an average and hit 29 centuries. He flourished until his record was surpassed by Sunil Gavaskar. His score of 334 runs against England in 1930 is a record. He became captain of the Australian cricket team in 1936.

Playing piano is a hobby with Bradman, who has now retired. "Farewell to Cricket" is the autobiography of this author of several books on cricket.

23. POET LAUREATE DANTE

Born in 1265 in Italy, Dante gained fame as the national poet of that country. Though he was born in a very poor family, he never forgot literature and did not give up writing. At that time, there was no scope in Italy to think freely or to speak or write what one felt.

He was branded as a revolutionary and banished from his land in 1302. He did not return to his motherland until death. But despite living in an alien nation, his love for his motherland did not diminish. He expressed his patriotism through his poetry. He died in 1321. "Divine Comedy" is his renowned work.

24. MIKHAIL GORBACHEV

Mikhail Gorbachev, who won the Nobel prize for peace, was President of the Soviet Union. He was not only a leader of the Union of Soviet Socialist

Republics, but also a symbol of democracy and a fearless and free world.

Born on March 2, 1931, Gorbachev became a graduate in law and agricultural science by his own effort. He is an idealist, optimist and a mild fighter. At the age of 59, he achieved his goal without giving scope for violence during the East European revolt, amidst threats and pressures of his countrymen. He played a direct role in the peaceful revolutions of East Germany and Czechoslovakia.

He ascended to power in March 1985 and demonstrated what all a determined leader can achieve in just five years. His policies of glasnost and perestroika created an atmosphere of liberalism in the Soviet society. They eventually resulted in breakup of the Soviet Union. He proved the feasibility of unifying the capitalist and the communist blocks of the world.

Gorbachev was the second leader to secure the Nobel prize for peace after American President Theodore Roosevelt won it in 1906. Another Russian who won the Nobel prize is Andrei Sakharav, physicist.

Gorbachev's contribution to end arms race to establish peace and security in the world, is invaluable.

25. ARISTOTLE

Aristotle was the greatest philosopher of Greece. He was a student of Plato. Born at Stagira, Italy, in 384 B.C. he was inspired by his father, who was a physician at the royal court of Philip II, King of Macedonia. By 335 B.C. he started writing about biology. He joined Plato's Academy at the age of 17. As a student of philosophy, he assisted Plato in his research till 347 B.C.

The king of Macedonia invited Aristotle to teach his son, Alexander. Aristotle taught Alexander for some time. After assuming power as the king, Alexander returned to Athens. There, he opened his own school of philosophy called the Lycium Academy. Aristotle knew several subjects. A master of zoology, botany, physics, initial physical science, political science, economics, psychology, discussion and poetry, he wrote hundreds of books. But all his works are not available. He spent his entire life in teaching. "There is a difference between the educated and the illiterate, just as there is a variation between the living beings and the non-living ones," he stated.

He declared : "There is no dignity in obtaining awards. Real dignity lies in the fact whether we are qualified for awards".

He died in 322 B.C.

26. PLATO

Plato, who was born in 428 B.C. in a rich family of Athens, is known as "the father of the Western political philosophy". Teacher of Aristotle and student of Socrates, he left Athens on a world tour when Socrates was sentenced to death. After travelling through Europe and West Asia, he met Dioniceus, first king of Syracuse. He tried to reform the king through his ideals and imagination. Dioniceus was ill-treating his people, being a dictator. But, Plato failed in reforming him.

After returning to Athens, he established a school called "The Academy" and strove to turn out ideal citizens through it. Mathematics, politics and philosophy were taught there.

Kings who ruled during Plato's lifetime were incapable and wicked. Plato explained his ideals in "The Republic". It elucidates an ideal state and the concept of a philosopher-king, as well as rules of education. "Laws", "Statesman" and "Apology" are his other works.

Plato tried in vain to reform Dioniceus II. Ultimately, he revised his opinions. He continued to teach at The Academy until his death in 347 B.C.

27. SOCRATES

Socrates was born in 470 B.C. in Athens. His father was a sculptor. Socrates was ugly in appearance. He joined the army as a youth and fought in several wars for Athens. Xanthipe was his wife. There was no compatibility between them. Her nature was wicked. Moreover, she was always furious. Socrates was not contented in married life. He became a Philosopher.

He adopted the method of finding answers by questioning himself to find the truth. He used to question himself until deriving the correct answer. His unconventional ideas angered the government. Though Socrates was very intelligent, people were not willing to accept his sayings. He began to say that "Ruling over the country is an art. All do not gain that knowledge. Everyone will not be competent to rule over a country". He questioned the existence of gods who were being worshipped traditionally in Athens. He did not concede the government's demand that he should withdraw his statements. The government sentenced him to death by forcing him to drink poison, baselessly accusing him of misleading youths by his thoughts. He died happily by consuming poison for the sake of his thoughts and beliefs. He lived till 400 B.C.

A famous quotation from Socrates is: "Beauty is short- lived". He also said: "A husband turns a philosopher if wife is wayward". His life illustrates the truth in his sayings.

28. GEORGE WASHINGTON

George Washington was born on February 11, 1732 in Virginia state. After working in 1749 as a surveyor of land, he joined the army. He became a Major in 1752 and gained fame. He completed his tour of about 1887 miles in the southern states in a horse carriage in 1761.

In 1775, he was appointed the Commander-in-Chief of the American colonies' armies which were ready to fight the British. He was the leader of America's freedom struggle. He was honoured by Americans as the "Father of the Nation." United States of America (U.S.A.) attained independence on July 4, 1776. In 1787, he became President of the Philadelphia conference which was convened to draft the new Republic's Constitution. The Constitution was formulated the same year. He assumed power as the first President of the U.S.A. on April 30, 1789. He stepped down in 1797. He passed away on December 14, 1799.

The Capital of U.S.A. is named after him as a mark of respect to him.

29. JOHN.F.KENNEDY

John Fitzerald Kennedy was very popular as President of the United States of America. He was born on May 29, 1917 in Boston. His father, Joseph Kennedy, was a business expert and politician. He studied at the Harvard University and became a graduate in 1940. He joined the American Navy in 1943. He was made a Commander for saving the lives of some persons during World War II. After the war, he entered politics and was elected to the House of Representatives in 1946.

In 1952, he was elected to the American Senate. In

1960, he contested election to the President and won after defeating his opponent, Richard Nixon.

As President, Kennedy declared that America would not hesitate to use nuclear arms if the Soviet Union did not withdraw missiles from Cuba. The bold steps taken by him during the Cuban missile crisis is remarkable.

He was a good author. Both "Profiles in Courage" and "Why England Slept" are popular books written by him. He had received the Pulitzer prize. He always supported the aspirations of youth.

On November 23, 1963 J.F. Kennedy fell to a bullet fired by an assassin while driving along with his wife to deliver a public speech in Dallas. The apostle of peace had a violent death. With his dastardly killing, a great statesman of the world eclipsed.

30. ADOLF HITLER

Adolf Hitler, who was born on April 20, 1889, had begun to earn a living as an artist after dropping out of school at the age of 16. During World War I, he joined the army and fought. In 1919, he joined the German Labour Party. Later, it was known as the Nazi Party. He was appointed the Chancellor of Germany in 1933. It was a great position attained by him. But he soon became a dictator.

In 1936, Austria annexed Phineland from France and merged with Germany. In 1939, German forces occupied Czechoslovakia. When they surrounded

Poland in September, World War II commenced. Though Hitler won in the beginning, he had to taste defeat on surrounding the Soviet Union in 1941. On learning about annihilation of the German army, unable to accept his defeat, he committed suicide on April 30, 1945.

However, it is interesting to note that inspite of causing so much bloodshed and wars, he led a simple life. He was a vegetarian and kind to children and animals. He caused the death of about 50 million people by drawing countries of the world to World War II. Hitler was a great victor. None else has influenced world history as much as he did.

31. SIR WINSTON CHURCHILL

Sir Winston Leonard Spencer Churchill was one of the foremost personalities of the 20th century. His command over English language was exceptional. That was his forte.

He was born on November 30, 1874 as the son of Lord Randolph Churchill. His mother was an American. His father was a political expert. Churchill could not study much. He remained very dull at school. As it did not suit him, he joined the army. He was in Bangalore (India) for some time. Later, he went to South Africa and worked as a war correspondent of the "Morning Post" in 1899. The Boer War was being fought then. Churchill was arrested. Somehow, he escaped and fled to England. He was elected to Parliament. He became a minister in 1906 and the First Lord in 1911. He was the Colonial Secretary from 1921 to 1923.

At the critical time of World War II, Churchill was invited to lead the all-party government. He served very successfully. When he was the Prime Minister of England, not only Britain, but the entire Europe had to face invasion by the Nazi group of Germany. Churchill was a formidable administrator. He roared that he would not surrender, but face the enemy. At last, he won after six years. Nazi leader Hitler suffered defeat.

The world cannot forget Churchill's famous deeds. He was a veteran author. "The World Crisis" and "Gathering Storm and Aftermath" are his very popular works. He wrote his "Memoirs of World War II" in six volumes. He was presented the Nobel Prize for literature for this work in 1953.

Churchill breathed his last on January 24, 1965. His reputation will remain for ever for his leadership during World War II.

32. PABLO PICASSO

Pablo Rooji Picasso was born on October 5, 1881 in Spain. He imbibed the art of painting rapidly from his childhood itself, due to an environment of artists at home. His father, Jose Rooji Picasso, was a drawing teacher. Pablo Picasso was a born artist. He could draw most beautiful pictures at the age of nine. He devoted his entire life to art and its development.

In 1904, he married Fernando Olivier.

In 1906, Picasso joined Brock to formulate a new style of drawing called "cubism". He brought into practice his own method in sculpting. He had studied not only drawing, but also its different forms like sculpture, ceramics, graphic arts and theatre design. He produced 13,500 paintings. He has drawn more than 30,000 sketches. He has the distinction of making 400 sculptures.

"Two Brothers" and seated "Harlequins" are invaluable works of Picasso. In 1901, he painted a sketch of himself. It was sold for six lakh dollars in New York in 1921. He was 40 years of age then. "Gurnica" produced by him in 1937, illustrates violence in Spain's civil war. This is his most notable work.

Picasso died at the age of 91 years in 1972. He was reputed as the greatest artist of the 20th century. Today, study of Picasso's paintings is very important for other artists.

33. DANIEL DEFOE

Daniel Defoe was a great author. He was born in 1660 in London. His father, Foe, was a mutton merchant. Defoe is considered as the originator of English composition. "Robinson Crusoe", written by him, is world-famous. Though he has written several other novels, this earned a unique position to him in the literary world. This is a work based on the experiences of Alexander Selkirk, a discoverer from Scotland, who had to remain on a deserted island off the Chilean coast on the Pacific Ocean. Defoe wrote so nicely that the reader identifies himself with his narration. This work has been translated into many languages of the world. He was interested in journalism also. In 1704, he brought out a journal called "The Review." He was known as a daring reviewer. His uniqueness was that he stated what he wanted, without fearing anyone. He suffered a lot due to this. He was imprisoned. But indefatigable Defoe became a model in journalism. He died in 1731. His other notable works which are worth reading are: Mall Fraunders, Roxana, The History of Life and Adventures of Mr. Duncan Campbell, and A Journal of the Plague War.

34.ALFRED NOBEL

It would be difficult to imagine a greater contradiction than was summed up in the life and work of Alfred Nobel, the insignificant-looking Swede who yearned for world peace-- and became a multi-millionaire by selling the weapon of death to each and every country which would pay his price for it. Alfred Nobel died working to invent a force of total destruction--and yet, ironically, his last will and testament laid down the terms of an imaginative effort to end all wars: the Nobel Prize.

Alfred Bernhard Nobel was the scientist who established the Nobel Prize Foundation. Born in 1833 in Stockholm, he became a scientist like his father, Immanuel Nobel. He led a bachelor's life and produced dynamite. It was invented accidentally.

One day, he observed a little nitro-glycerine which had been dropped from a flask at his laboratory. That liquid fell on fine soil powder kept in a box. It did not explode. Instead, it became a paste. He made a ball of that paste and exploded it outside effectively. Nobel, who devised a method to contain nitro-glycerine safely, called it "dynamite". He soon became very rich after inventing it. He executed a will in 1890 that the interest on 90,00,000 dollars should be presented every year to persons who serve humanity in science, literature and peace. Earlier, Nobel prize was being presented for physics, chemistry, medicine and physiology, literature and world peace only. In 1969, the Swedish Government announced that an Alfred Nobel Memorial Prize for economics will also be presented.

The Nobel prize is the largest of its kind in the world. Today, his reputation rests, not on his inventive genius, but on the international awards which bear his name. The story of Alfred Nobel is a story of a man "from rags to riches".

On 10, December, 1896, his butler who was alone in the house with him, found his millionaire master dead at his desk. Inside the desk, beneath a pile of designs for a new war weapon, lay his last will and testament of peace.

The will directed that his capital should become a fund, the annual interest on which was to be split into five equal parts and used to award prizes to the persons adjudged to have made the most important discovery or invention in the fields of physics, chemistry, physiology or medicine; the person who had produced the outstanding work of literature, "idealistic in character"; and to the person who has done the most or best work for the brotherhood of nations, the abolition of standing armies as well as the formation or popularization of peace congresses".

However, now that scientists have really found out a more destructive atomic bomb, the world hopes that his aim to make the war impossible, will now be realised, because the atomic bomb has become a deterrent weapon and while many have it, every nation is afraid of it!

35. WALT DISNEY

It is now not extraordinary that pictures sketched by a person, play, dance and act on the screen. But, it was Walt Disney who first demonstrated such a phenomena. He was born in 1901 in Chicago in a poor family. Though he was fond of drawing pictures in his childhood, be began life as a labourer, fearing that his hobby would not help him earn a living.

During World War II, he came to France and worked as a driver of an ambulance van. Just then, the world was getting interested in the art of drawing cartoons. Disney, who had mastered this art, earned money by drawing cartoons on glass at an advertising company. He returned to America and started making movies along with his brothers at Hollywood. He aspired to make a film in which cartoon characters depicted by him would act.

At first, he succeeded by making cartoon films as small movies. Later, he made cartoon films of long duration. His cartoon films became a craze all over the world. Mickey Mouse created by him is as dear to children as chacolates.

Disneyland created by Disney in America so as to enrich children's knowledge, is world-famous.

Disney died in 1966. He was renowned as an artist throughout his life.

36. MAX MUELLER

The German scholar, Max Mueller, was very fond of India. He studied the Vedas and Sanskrit literature for over 50 years, He brought out an outstanding book, "Sacred Books of the East," in several volumes.

He was born in 1823 at Thessa. While studying at the Leipzig University, he learnt a lot about India and its books. He studied the Vedas and the Upanishads extensively. But it is interesting that he did not visit India at all. "I did not desire to see India. But I have understood the heart of that country very well", he said.

Now, Max Mueller Bhavans in leading cities of India are functioning as bridges between Germany and India. Max Mueller lived for 80 years.

37. EARNEST HEMINGWAY

Earnest Hemingway was born on July 21, 1899 in America. But he lived mostly outside America.

He was an ordinary vehicle driver. He crossed over to journalism and became a newspaper correspondent.

He was a talented novelist of the 20th century. Before delving into writing, he served in the military also during the World War. He lamented human behaviour and the violent acts in the war. He gained good experience in the military. All three novels--"Man without Woman", "The Sun Also Rises" and "A Farewell to Arms"--are all on war.

Hemingway's other novels are: "Across the River and the Trees", "Death in the Afternoon", "The Old Man and the Sea", "For Whom the Bell Tolls" and "Green Hills of Africa". He received the Nobel prize in

1954 for his book "The Old Man and the Sea". This novel bagged the Pulitzer prize also.

However, he committed suicide on July 2, 1961.

38. LENIN

Vladimir Illyitch Uliyanov was born on April 22, 1870 in Volga city of Simbirsk in Russia as the son of Iliya Uliyanov. He evinced interest in literature, history and linguistics. He knew several modern European languages. Well known as a revolutionary of the twentieth century, he called himself secretly as Lenin. Later he gained fame by that name only.

Lenin was influenced by reading the works of Marx and Engels. He indulged in political activities even as a student of Kajan University. Russia was ruled by the Tsars then. The Tsars drove him to different places on observing his efforts for social reforms and equality. Inspite of deportation, he continued his revolutionary struggle against the Tsar administration.

In 1898, he started the Bolshevik Party and initiated the Communist revolution in Russia. By 1917, he gave a shape to his revolution and imagination of Marx and Engels. A revolution by

Lenin flopped in 1905. He even edited two journals called Iskra and Proletary.

In 1917, Lenin's revolution succeeded and the new Soviet government was constituted under his leadership. The rule of eight hours' work per day for labourers was implemented at that time. This came into practice in all factories. Lenin, who was honoured by Russians as " The Founder of the Soviet Union", died on January 21, 1921 at Gorky near Moscow.

39. ROBERT MALTHUS

Robert Malthus was born as the second son of Daniel Malthus on February 14, 1766 in England. Daniel had eight children of whom six were daughters.

In 1782, Malthus gained friendship of Gilbert Wakefield and this paved the way for a smoother life for him in the future. In 1788 he became a graduate in mathematics. In 1791 he left Cambridge and joined as an assistant priest at Albary.

He studied the works of William Godwin and Marquis Decandorset, a revolutionary, and expressed his conclusions through an essay as follows:

"Population is increasing limitlessly. It is hampering happiness and peace of the people, without providing them proper food and accommodation . If rise in population is not stalled, man will be in difficulty, unable to live happily. Therefore, population and utilities required by those people to live well should be mutually equal".

Some optimists who read the essay on society's development being stalled by unlimited rise in population, denounced Malthus. Undeterred, he travelled all over Europe in 1799 and studied the level of population. There is no harm in taking care to see that population does not increase. He argued that evils, self- betrayal and sorrow will increase among people if population is not controlled.

In 1804, he became a professor of history and political economics at the East India College, Hailbury. He married at that time. He had three children. He could live happily in his final years thanks to two of them. He passed away on December 24, 1834.

Malthusianism, Malthusling and Malthusian philosophy are assets provided by Malthus to the world. He had mentioned 200 years ago, what we are now stating as family planning. He shaped the way for change in human thinking by solving himself a problem which arises from within him. The Malthusian theory of population is the first attempt in the world at controlling the numbers.

40. LOUIS PASTEUR

Louis Pasteur was a renowned scientist of France. Born in 1822, he evinced interest in nature, drawing and science from his childhood. A patriot, he became a member of the French Academy. He was noted for his scientific research. His service in the fields of medicine and chemistry have been lauded as unparalleled. His discoveries include: an infection as

a cause for cold; treatment for rabies disease caused by bite of mad dog and diseases like chicken pox. He discovered that milk turns sour by the presence of bacteria. He stated that bacteria can be destroyed by heating a little and that milk products like butter can be preserved for longer periods.

Worms and insects which cause diseases like tuberculosis can be eradicated by this special method. This method of keeping milk free from germs is called as Pasteurisation. The practice of preserving milk by Pasteurisation is prevalent in dairies.

Pasteur died at the age of 73, in 1895.

41. MAXIM GORKY

Born in 1868, Maxim Gorky was a famous writer of the Soviet Union. He was born at Nigani Nomgorad. His original name was Alexi Maximonich Peshkov. Orphaned in childhood, he was brought up by his mother's father. But he was cruel and stingy. So he had to work hard as a boy. Once he even worked in a footwear shop. Yet, he did not stop reading whenever he was free. It was a restriction for him. In order to utilise his knowledge, he became a journalist. He toured many places in Russia. The wretched condition of his people transformed him as a revolutionary and he enrolled as a member of the Communist Party.

In 1905, the Tsar Government not only arrested, but also deported him. But he did not give up his revolutionary activities. He was the head of the publicity section during the October Revolution of Russia in 1917.

Gorky means, 'bitter'. 'Mother' is his well-known work. This novel is translated into several languages of the world. He has depicted here, the life of ordinary people, which he had observed from close quarters, in a down-to-earth manner. "Lower Depth", "My childhood," and "Reminiscences" are some of his other works. He had ample love for his country. Russians have immense respect for Gorky, who passed away in 1936.

42. MICHAEL FARADAY

Michael Faraday was born on September 22, 1791 at Nevington Butts village on the banks of the Thames river. This was very much a part of London. His father's job was to fix metal shoes to horses' hooks. He could not educate his son by that profession. Faraday dropped out of the school at the age of

13. He joined work at a book-shop. He had to sweep the floor on reaching the shop in the morning, wipe windows and doors, deliver daily newspapers and bind books rest of the time. Science books were being received there often for binding. He read some of them. He was not only reading curiously, but also noting down important topics noticed in them.

He was attending science meets which were being held there often. He was making notes on various discoveries by scientists. He bound the notes written by him. A book bound thus is preserved at the Royal Institute's Library in London.

Faraday became a scientist on his own. He demonstrated to the world the truth that electricity can be produced from stone power. The entire world is indebted to this great scientist. Dynamos and generating units at the generating stations which we see today, are his contributions. The inventor of the generation died on August 25, 1867.

43. GUSTAV EIFFEL

Gustav Eiffel was born in France in 1832. He prospered as a great technologist. His advice as constructor of the world- famous bridge of France to instal a 300-metre high steel tower to commemorate the World Fair held by a batch of industrialists in Paris in 1880, was accepted.

Its work commenced in January 1887. Eiffel

invited several engineers and designers. They worked non-stop for two years. Eiffel strove very hard for the construction. Over 25,00,000 rivets were used to join 15,000 steel parts. Four huge arches were erected on about 10,000 square metres of land. 250 persons worked on the project, Many criticised him on seeing the tower under construction. Eiffel did not relent at all. The project was completed in 1889. It was called the Eiffel Tower.

Other structures by Eiffel, who was an expert in steel and concrete constructions, were Mariapia bridge in Portugal, the foundation required for the Statue of Liberty in New York and other structures of steel.

Now, the Eiffel Tower is 100 years old. It has remained firm and immortalised Eiffel's name. He died on December 27, 1923 at the age of 91. Rarely does a visitor to Paris return without seeing the world-famous Eiffel Tower.

44. HOMER

Poet Homer is presumed to have lived in the 9th century B.C. He was blind and used to roam ancient Greece narrating stories and singing. Though people of many countries did not care for him while he was alive, they scrambled to identify themselves with him after he passed away. He was a great poet. Poems sung by him constituted two works of poetry called Iliad and Odyssey. Both these poems are considered invaluable in the world of literature. Several poets were inspired by these poems. Iliad depicts the Trojan war which spanned over 10 years. Odyssey has 10 years itinerary of Odysias, a Greek commander, as its theme. Both these poems throw light on the life of the Greeks at that time. Homer has become immortal through them.

45. CHARLES DARWIN

Charles Robert Darwin was born in 1809 in England. His father was a doctor. Darwin studied at Shrewsbury, Edinburgh and Cambridge. His father wanted him to become a doctor. But Darwin had evinced interest in history, nature and Geology. He began to conduct research as a scientist.

In 1831, he got an opportunity to tour the world in a ship called "The Beagale". He travelled till 1836, studying living beings in different parts of the world. When he reached South America, he compared living beings there with those in England. Thus, he made a thorough study of flowers, animals and rock fossils. He studied the mode of man's evolution and wrote a book "Origin of Species" in 1859. "Descent of Man" is his other work.

According to him, for these living beings (including

human being) of today to assume this appearance, evolution over several thousand years is the reason. He discovered that monkey is the origin of man or man has evolved from Monkey. Darwin was a great geographical discoverer too.

"Evolution of Man" is his greatest contribution to biological science. He died on April 19, 1882.

46. MAO TSE-TUNG

Mao Tse-tung was born on December 26, 1893 in Hunan, southern province of China. Since his was a farmer's family, he had to experience extreme poverty. Reading was his hobby from childhood. After the great Chinese Revolution, he indulged in revolutionary activities against the Manchur dynasty (1911).

Following the fall of Communist rule in Soviet Land under the leadership of Lenin, Mao established the Chinese Communist Party in 1921. In 1930, he established the Chinese Soviet Republic at Kiangsi. But the government prohibited them. Then Mao started the historic walk and reached Yenan in north-west China by travelling 3,000 miles along with his followers. Mao suffered terribly during this journey.

After Japan's defeat in World War II, Mao declared China as a People's Republic around 1949. He initiated steps to reconstruct China, along with friends like Chou-en Lai. He even succeeded in facing anti-Communist forces. His countrymen started worshipping him like God. He spent his complete life to establish Communist China. He died on September 9, 1976. Later, his opponents renounced his principles. But the revolution launched by Mao has remained as a historic truth.

47. ALEXANDER DUMAS

World-famous novelist, Alexander Dumas, was born in 1802. Writing was his hobby. He mastered the art of writing novels and remained a novelist throughout his life. "Three Musketeers" is the greatest novel of this French citizen. This is a historical novel. "The Count of Monte Christo", "Black Tulp", and "The Man in the Iron Mask" are some of his other novels. He excelled in telling stories.

"Three Musketeers" has been translated into innumerable languages of the world. This novel depicts the life of three soldiers who struggled to uphold truth. This novel hit the screen also as a movie.

48. ZARATHUSTRA

Zarathustra caused advent of a religion. This religion observed by the Parsees underscores compassion, love and tolerance. Zarathustra lived in 600 B.C. It is said, he realised God when he was only 15 years of age. He enunciated two main influences called Ahurmajda and Ahiraman. Ahurmajda means light and divine form. Ahiraman means darkness or violent form. Though he converted kings like Vishatalpa, as one who had realised Ahurmajda, he was killed by an irreligious king. But he never gave up religion.

He was the founder of Zorastrianism and the Parsee religion.

49. YEHUDI MENUHIN

Yehudi Menuhin was born in 1916 in a Jewish family in New York. He learnt to play violin at the age of just five and became a world-famous violin maestro. (T.Chowdiah of Karnataka and Lalgudi Jayaraman of Tamil Nadu are renowned violinists of India). He very much likes Indian music. His role in popularising Indian music in the West is noteworthy. He visited India in response to a request by Pandit Jawaharlal Nehru and conducted his symphony in prominent cities here.

Credit goes to him for having invited B.K.S. Iyengar, India's well-known practitioner of yogasanas and yoga teacher, to Western countries, as a result of which music maestros like Malcoo Jinski, Crifford Curzon and Nikita Khruschev became his students. It is notable that B.K.S.Iyengar helped Yehudi Menuhin when he was unable to play on his violin, by setting right his fingers through practising yogasanas.

50. JOSEPH STALIN

Joseph Stalin, who was born in 1879 in Georgia, is a very popular personality in Russia, after Lenin. A politician of the Soviet Union, he was the leader of Russians for 30 years. A revolutionary at the age of 17, he played a very important role in the war which took place after 1917. He led the military in a war against Germany in June 1941. He was criticised severely by the Russian leaders. He died on March 5, 1953. Stalin means a man of steel.

51. BERTRAND RUSSEL

Born on May 12, 1872, Bertrand Russel was a renowned British philosopher and mathematician. He was also an eminemt writer. "The Conquest of Happiness", "In praise of Idleness", "Principia Mathematica", which is a masterpiece in three volumes, "Religion and Science"., etc., are works written by him. He strove immensely in politics also. He served as a professor in institutions like the California University and the New York College. He received the Nobel prize for literature in 1950.

A controversial person, he was a great thinker. His thoughts are influential even now. He passed away on February 2, 1970. Eight months prior to his death, he had opposed the Russian Prime Minister, Kosygin, for expelling Alexander Solzenitsm from the

Soveit Writers' Federation. He was 97 years old then. This greatest thinker of the 20th century, was also an orator.

52. HELEN KELLER

Helen Keller was born on June 27, 1880 at Tusumbia in Alabama. Arthur Keller was her father and Catherine, her mother. Helen Keller became blind and deaf at the tender age of 19 months. She could not see or hear anything.

While reading American Notes by Charles Dickens, Catherine gathered that the Perkins Institute in Boston served blind people and that Samuel Gridley Howe had successfully taught reading and writing to another girl like Helen Keller. Michael Anagos of Greece was the chief of that institution. Catherine contacted Ani Sullivan there and arranged for education to Helen Keller.

Helen not only learnt English, Latin, Greek, French and German through the Braille script, but also started to converse through the language of finger signs. She passed the B.A., examination at Raddiff College in 1900. She wrote two books--"Optimism" and "The Story of My life" while at college. She contributed articles to newspapers. In an article, she mentioned that drops of silver nitrate should be put on a just- born infant's eyes to prevent blindness by infection.

In 1918, a Holywood cinema company approached Helen to make a film called "Deliverance". Although that film failed as a drama, some of its scenes were used in a successful film, "The Unconquered", 40 years later. Ani and Helen used to deliver lectures. Helen strove hard to earn money to become self-reliant.

Helen joined the American Blind People's Foundation in 1923. She was a pillar of strength to those who had lost their eyes in war. Despite blindness, she was conducting herself well like a sighted person. During World War II, she inspired air force personnel and soldiers who were injured in the eye, by meeting them. She strove for the blind people for half a century. She died on June 1, 1968 at the age of 88. Her achievement is unique.

53. GIUSEPPE GARIBALDI

Giuseppe Garibaldi was born on July 4, 1807 as the son of Giuseppe, Captain of the Garibaldi ship. He grew up as a famous soldier and patriot of Italy. Following his arrest for hatching a conspiracy to seize a government ship, he was sentenced to death in 1934. But, he escaped and fled to South America. After some time, he returned to Italy and became the chief of a large service army. He struggled to free Italy from shackles. He died in 1882.

54. HUYEN-TSANG

Huyen-tsang was a pilgrim of China to India. He not only visited the royal court of Harshavardhan in India between 606 and 647 A.D., but also recorded his observations of India. His writings have provided several interesting information about India, of those times.

55. FLORENCE NIGHTINGALE

Renowned as the "Lady with the lamp", Florence Nightingale was born in 1820 in Florence, Italy. She could have led an easy life as desired by her parents. But she studied nursing in Germany and France and wanted to remain a nurse throughout her life. She served as the leader of a 40-member team to the British Army Hospital during the Crimean War between 1854 and 1856. This hospital was situated at Scutari in Turkey. Here, she served the injured persons at her own expense. She used to hold a lamp in her hand while visiting her patients. So she was known as "The lady with the lamp." She not only opened a nursing school at the St.Thomas Hospital, London, but also encouraged women to join the medical profession.

Prior to her, British hospitals lacked any nursing facilities. She was a pioneer and initiated modern nursing arrangement. Known for kindness and sacrifice, she died in 1910 at London.

56. NAPOLEAN BONAPARTE

Napolean Bonaparte was a famous French statesman. Born in 1776, he grew up as a hero and became the emperor after the great French Revolution. He struggled against England, Russia and Austria in 1805 and won consecutively all those wars. But he suffered defeat in the Waterloo War in June 1815. He was deported to St. Helena. He died there six years thereafter.

57. SIR ISAAC NEWTON

Sir Isaac Newton, a famous scientist, was born in 1642 in an ordinary farmer's family of England. After obtaining the B.A. degree from Trinity College, Cambridge, he engaged himself in scientific research. He had evinced interest in science from his childhood. At that time, he devised a clock which works with the aid of water. Newton is the most outstanding among scientists produced by Britain. His aim was to achieve scientific progress through experiments. Influenced by Galileo, a renowned scientist, Newton is noted in the world of science by his research like law of movement, law of heaviness, mobility and conveyance of light. He also made reflective telescopes which could be an easy instrument for studying asteroids.

Elucidation of earth's relativity is the research that gained fame for Newton. Even its detection accidentally was a miracle. One day, he saw an apple falling to the ground from the tree. Through this, he realised that earth has the power of relativity by which it attracts things towards it. He used this theory to know the movement of stars and planets in the solar system.

Newton's scientific discovery and theories are published in his book, "Principia." He was the first scientist to receive the Knighthood ("Sir" award). The Royal Society of London elected him as its Fellow and appointed him as its life-chairman. He died in 1722. He was known as a kind-hearted person. He had qualities like patience and forbearance which a scientist should have.

58. JESUS CHRIST

Jesus Christ established the Christian religion which has the highest number of followers in the world. He was born in 04 B.C. at Bethlehem near Jerusalem. His father was Joseph and his mother, Mary. Theirs was a very poor family.

Jesus Christ evinced

interest in religious topics from childhood. He read Hebrew religious books. At the age of 30, he gave up carpentry and began to propagate religion. His objective was to achieve universal brotherhood. But Pilata, Governor of Rome, considered that it was opposed to traditionally known Hebrew theories. He ordered that Christ be killed by piercing nails into him on the Calvary Hill.

Though Christ died by ascending the cross and getting nailed to it, he did not get angry even a little against those who subjected him to punishment. Instead, he breathed his last by praying: "Lord, they are making a mistake without knowing what they are doing. Pardon them". He passed away in 33 A.D.

An embodiment of love and compassion, Christ was a messenger of peace. He had several lakh disciples. His teachings and stories are included in the New Testament. He led a simple and pitiable life. He was a man of miracles.

59. LEONARDO DA VINCI

Leonardo, who was born at Vinci, Italy in 1452, was a great savant. Noted as a painter, scientist, technologist and musician, he devised scientific methods which would facilitate study of geography and astronomy. Odometre, magic lantern and wrench are some of the instruments developed by him. He had produced models of printing machines, mills, etc. This is a rare painting in the entire history. He strove

immensely for rejuvenating Italy.

The Mona Lisa painting is preserved at the Louvre Museum in Paris. Innumerable people have seen it. "Last Supper" and "Madonna" are other notable paintings by Vinci. He died in 1519. He was an exceptional genius of the 16th century.

60. GALLON

Gallon, who studied medical science systematically, is called "The father of human anatomy". He said, only truth should be spoken and listened to. He spent his life in search of truth. He loved nature and said he would "not resort to action without purpose of nature". Symptoms of illness are not a way to some dangerous diseases, but they are also beneficial to us, he said. His book, "Art of medicine", was the basic text-book for medical students till the 16th Century.

Born at Pergamum in Asia Minor, he travelled in Greece and Rome. He died at Cicily. His methods of medical treatment are guides even now.

61. HIPPOCRATES

Hippocrates is called "The father of naturopathy". He was a teacher for doctors. Hippocrate's oath is the ideal for those taking up the medical profession.

Born in 490 B.C. at Cass Island of Greece, he followed nature which is helpful in the treatment of illness. " A doctor can only co-operate," he said. He used to visit his patients' houses and return after rendering medical treatment. He has stated his conclusions in small sentences which are popular, like "Do not work when you are hungry", "Eat more in winter, and less in summer". Many such quotations can be remembered easily.

Paracelsus (of Switzerland), Vincent Preesnitz (who treated with water), Looni Kuhne (author of "The New Science of Healing"), Henry Lind Laher (author of "The Philosophy of Nature Cure") and others, are well-known naturopaths like Hippocrates.

62. GEORGE STEPHENSON

There were several scientists like Marie Curie, Alexander Fleming, Henrico Fermin and Galileo. Likewise, some are technocrats. George Stephenson is one among them. Henry Ford, Good Year among others, made several inventions.

Stephenson is known as "The father of the railways." Born in 1781, he was the son of a fireman in a coal mine. Stephenson also was working at the mine along with his father and studying at leisure time. While working at the mine, an idea of running an engine occurred to him. In 1814, he succeeded in making a locomotive which could pull trucks carrying coal. In 1825, he produced the first passenger train of the world. In 1830, a railway line was laid from Liverpool to Manchester. A tube- shaped boiler engine fabricated by Stephenson pulled the train on it. It was called "Rocket".

Stephenson not only devised engines, but also several railways were laid under his leadership.

His contributions to the world of railways is laudable. He will always be remembered as the inventor of railway which is a major means of transport of goods and people in the world.

Stephenson died in the year 1848.

63. MARIE CURIE

Marie Curie, the Polish-born French scientist had the rare honour of receiving two Nobel Prizes and that too for different discoveries.

Born in the year 1867, in a very proud family of an academician, she studied under difficult circumstances and obtained her Masters in her favourite subjects--physics and mathematics. She married Pierre in Paris. Incidentally, Pierre was also a physicist who announced the discovery of Piezo-electricity. In 1903, she shared the Nobel Prize in Physics with Pierre Curie and Henri Becquerel. Later, in the year 1911, she won the Nobel Prize in chemistry. The 1911 prize was awarded to her for her services for the advancement of chemistry by the discovery of the elements--Radium and Polonium and also for the isolation of characterization of the element Radium and its compounds.

Radium is being constantly formed in nature by the radioactive decay of uranium. Radium releases large amounts of high-energy radiation which can be harmful to human health. It tends to accumulate in the bones where it destroys the tissues that produce red blood cells, and can cause bone cancer. However, radium salts can also be used for treatment of cancer.

Using tons of Uranium ore mass, she was able to isolate a tenth of a gramme of pure radium. She also pioneered in some of the earliest medical applications of X-rays and Radium.

Till today, Radium therapy remains one of the major treatments for the dreaded cancer. As irony would have it, she died of blood cancer as a result of exposure to radiation herself, in the year 1934.

64. MARCO POLO

Marco Polo was a geographical discoverer. He was an adventurist. Like Columbus who discovered America during his voyage in 1498 A.D., Marco Polo was the first European who visited China. Through China, he also visited India and other eastern countries. Born in 1256 in Venice, he lived for 75 years. He took up discovery even before Columbus.

Likewise, other discoverers are Magellan (world tour), Amundson (South Pole), Sebastin(Newfoundland), James Cook (New Zealand), Tasman (Tasmania), Neil Armstrong (voyage to the Moon) and Vasco da Gama (sea route to India).

65. H.G. WELLS

H.G. Wells was born in the year 1866 in England in a family at the extreme lower edge of a lower middle class. The speciality of Wells is that he became a writer of international repute, having been brought up and lived in that special strata of the lower middle class, which, in his time, were superior servants.

Wells' father was an under-gardener, but not a successful one even in that job because he lost that also and had to make some sort of living out of professional cricket (in those days, another form of domestic service). He also made a pathetic attempt to run a shop. He made a very bad living, and for most of Wells' part, did not have enough to eat. His mother began life as a ladies' maid and was later a house-keeper in a large and aristocratic house.

Author of scientific romances, such as "The First Men on the Moon" and "The War of the Worlds", he invented more literary devices than most people do in their whole careers.

Between the years 1900 and 1914, Wells made a whole set of practical prophesies, including the concepts of the tank and the military aircraft. That kind of foresight he shared with Churchill, for whom he had great regard and admiration. It was mutual.

Wells was a very curious, impersonal and little man and used to make fun of his own diminutive figure. He never cared for what others thought of him. He was quite often bad-tempered, irritable and indifferent to audience. Yet, he wrote some of the best novels of the world--"Tono Bungay", "Kipps," and "Love and Mr. Lewisham".

His book, "The Time Machine" is a master-piece. Wells dreamt of a new vision and a new society with new enlightenment --a society founded on science. He thought that poverty, hunger and the material miseries of the poor, were an insult to man's intelligence. A good deal of his social thinking reads quite fresh nowadays.

In his autobiography, he said that he wanted to commit suicide at the age of 16 years. He slept on the top floor of his house, while bombs were being dropped on London during the war.

Wells was optimistic about the war and his military judgments turned out right. His verbal gift was unquestionable.

However, his last years were not enviable. He wanted to be an F.R.S. (Fellow of the Royal Society, London), but could not. He was obsessed with this ambition. He had been the prophet of the 20th century science, more effectively than any man alive. Still he could not become an F.R.S.

Wells died in the year 1946 at the age of 80 years.

66. CONFUCIUS

Confucius was a Chinese philosopher whose main stress was on character. He was also a social reformer. Born at Shantung in the year 551 BC, he had to earn his bread from the early age of 8 years. He married at the age of 16.

Confucius's real name was Kung Futse. After marriage, he matured into a philosopher and started preaching his philosophical ideas and ideals to people. Later, he kept himself away from the mundane world and earthly temptations and lead a simple life like an ascetic. He died at the age of 71.

The main thrust of Confucian philosophy was individual character. He preached that children should respect their parents. Chinese people then, as now also, hold Confucius in high esteem as a great philosopher, thinker and social reformer.

Confucius occupied many high posts in China because of his accomplishments and self-less service to people. He prepared many plans for the eradication of poverty in China which was its greatest affliction.

He opened a school in which many people took lessons on leading a virtuous life. He was a master of many languages and arts. He has written about his experiences in life in a book entitled "Chin Chiuking".

Confucius came to wield so much influence in China that his thoughts attained the status of a religion. Actually, his thoughts became the official religion of China in 120 BC. Even to this day, many people follow his teachings and have great respect for their ancestors and lay stress on social morality and individual character. The Chinese people are, by and large, tradition-bound. Even with the passage of centuries since Confucius, the Chinese people have retained the eternal values of life which Confucius taught them.

It was the firm opinion of Confucius that morality should be the basis of society and religion. He suggested many ways to avoid class conflict. "Do not treat others in a manner that you would not like others to treat you," was his basic thought.

67. SOLOMON

For ages, King Solomon's name has been regarded as synonymous with wisdom. In fact, he is known as Solomon, the wise. Hundreds of stories circulate all over the world regarding his sense of justice. It was said that if King Solomon could not find a solution to a problem, it could never be solved.

A story runs: Two women, both claiming to be mothers of the same child, approached Solomon for justice. Solomon thought over the problem and asked the child to be cut into two pieces and one part each given to them. The real mother at once withdrew her claim and asked the King to give the child to the other woman. Solomon immediately ruled that she was the real mother as no mother would allow her child to be harmed let alone cut into two pieces. He gave the child to that woman.

Wisdom was the hallmark of Solomon's rule. He had no equal as far as governing his country was concerned. He built a huge temple in Jerusalem and passed laws to eradicate poverty. He knew many languages and could convert any enemy into a friend. He encouraged trade and made his kingdom prosperous. His era is described as the 'Golden age' in Jewish history. He nominated his son David as his successor, though his other sons revolted against his decision. He entered into matrimonial relations with neighbouring kingdoms to have friendly ties with them.

Much research is being done even now on Solomon. It is said that he had hidden treasure worth billions at some secret place. This treasure is supposed to be cursed and many people have lost their lives in trying to find it out.

68. JULIUS CAESAR

Born in the year 100 BC, Julius Caesar is one of the most remarkable personalities in world history. He is generally regarded as the greatest genius of ancient

Rome. He was really a man of exceptional and varied talents. He left an indelible mark on military leadership, statesmanship, oratory, writing, laws and administration during his time and after. He possessed great personal qualities too. He was handsome, witty, kind and forgiving.

The greatness of Caesar as a ruler and conqueror is indicated by the fact that all succeeding Roman emperors called themselves Caesars. Some empires of a later date gave their rulers titles derived from the name Caesar as 'Czars' of Russia and 'Kaisers' of Germany. When Caesar entered Roman politics, Roman empire was confined to the Mediterranean only, but by conquering France, Belgium and parts of Spain, he extended it up to Europe and laid the foundation of Western Europe as we know today.

The first forty years of Caesar's life was a troubled period in Roman political life. The republican system was crumbling and the state was torn by revolution and civil war. Up to this time, Caesar had not achieved much by way of political power except a few magisterial appointments and a command in Spain, but his ability in the battlefield was established and he also gained necessary political experience.

In 60 BC, Caesar made an attempt to gain real power. To achieve this objective, he befriended two leading generals of Rome, Pompey and Crassus, who were opposed to each other. Caesar arranged a patch-up between the two and with their help, established the First Triumvirate (three-man rule) in 60-54 BC. Thus, together with these two, he managed the affairs of Rome. Then, by his political shrewdness, won the election for Consul. During his term of office as Consul, Caesar introduced many important reforms. The next appointment that Caesar got was the commandership of Roman armies in Gaul for a period of five years.

During this period, Caesar led a number of brilliant and successful military campaigns. Caesar's life was cut short when he was murdered under a conspiracy at the theatre of Pompey on March 15, 44 BC. The conspirators were opposed to the one-man rule of Caesar and they also feared that Caesar might restore. Kingship in Rome for which Romans had a great aversion.

69. DAG HAMMARSKJOLD

Dag Hammarskjold was one of the greatest civil servants of the modern world. He was a very friendly, courteous, intelligent, and shrewd administrator on the world scene. He was born in the year 1905 in an aristocratic family of Sweden and was highly religious-minded.

As he grew up into an young man, Dag attained success after success, not only in his school and college, but also in his assignments. He was essentially a man of action and nobility.

Dag's worldly success was so smooth that no man could have aspired for anything better. Like some of the best minds of Sweden in those days, he turned to economics and soon became a good economist of his country. He went into an administrative job at the age of 25, but he aspired for power and a life of action. At the age of 30, he was appointed as the permanent secretary of the treasury.

Dag was not a socialist in the dogmatic sense of the word, but socialism was at his heart and mind all the time. At the age of 36, Dag became chairman of the Riksbank of Sweden, which was somewhat equivalent to the Bank of England in status, and the permanent secretary of the Treasury, at the same time.

At the age of 41, he became secretary-general of the foreign ministry, and later, a non-party member of the cabinet at the age of 46.

It was at this point of time that Dag was offered the secretary-generalship of the United Nations, at which he jumped and accepted the same. His was vanity mixed with nobility. He wanted to leave a mark on history and liked being a world- figure. He was in the thick of controversies as the secretary- general of the UN. He was at the centre-stage during the Suez crisis and the Congo war. He was caught in the cobweb of the politics of power among the major world powers. Yet, he came out unscathed as an able, unbiased and clean administrator of world politics.

Dag used to say: Without the U.N. where should we have been now? Anywhere else, but where we are! He said of himself once: " I am a kind of secular Pope". Dag was a symbol of international understanding and amity. Some say that his mission in world politics, was a 'heroic failure'. Dag could speak with complete fluency in four languages. He always thought that he was only an instrument of God in his service to humanity.

During the Suez crisis that gripped the world, Dag had to work for nearly 18 hours a day in the office, and he once said: "We should die with decency, so that at least decency will survive". He believed in literal terms that he would have to take his way along to suffering, shame and the sacrifice of his life." To him the only value of life was its content.

The secretary-generalship of the UN to Dag was never a bed of roses. It is not so even now, however. Any worldly man would have to think twice before accepting that post. Once, he was on the verge of quitting in humiliation. However, he survived both the Suez war and the Congo war.

Dag had indeed a premonition of his own death. He died in the year 1961 in an air crash on an official mission to Congo.

—— ooOoo ——